What Others

Echoing Silence fro...

The verse Romans 8:28 from scripture, "All things work together for good....." comes to life within the words of *Echoing Silence from the Child Within* as Shari shares her lifetime journey from the brokenness of generational abuse to the wholeness of mind, body, and soul. As a Registered Nurse of 33 years and one who believes in the approach of holistic healing, I have seen firsthand the *dis-ease* inflicted by abuse to the mind, body, and soul. While the role of medical professionals is brought in to intervene and discover the elusive cause of the manifested *dis-ease*, it is the truth that there is only One Who can truly heal the devastating consequences of abuse. I see the Light of freedom and healing shine in Shari's eyes as she speaks of it. She is as authentic as she is real. In her honesty and transparency, Shari shows how the compassionate and loving hand of God continually brings her through the process of healing to wholeness. Written to reach into the heart of anyone who has suffered abuse at the hand of another, there is truth and hope offered in this beautifully written, careful to digest, allegory. Whether you are the one abused, or you love one who has been abused, this book offers more than just hope. It offers the path to discover the process of healing and freedom, and ultimately, coming to know the Healer Himself. A must read for anyone who loves Life, or anyone who longs to love Life. For such a time as this, we need the Truth and helping Hand on the pathway to healing and wholeness.

-Jenny Cierley, RN, BSN

Shari has bravely written her own story to give a voice to the voiceless millions who are being trafficked in the worldwide sex trade. This is a must-read book for anyone who is ready to take their voice back.

-Christine Maier, Sergeant, NYPD, Ret., Author of *Blue Sky Morning*

Shari shows us that it is possible for every person who has been sexually abused to restore their voice and value as they realign to become the person God created them to be. With hope, healing is possible.

-Daphne V. Smith, Chain Breaker, Wave Maker, Coach, and Author of *What's YOUR Scarlet Letter?*

In *Echoing Silence from the Child Within,* you hear the voice of the stolen innocence of a child and the struggle of a woman to find her and start over with hope. As Shari opens her heart to the world, your heart will be opened to hear the need of so many girls to hear they are truly loved.

-Dow Tippett, Relational Arts Instructor, Business Leadership Coach, Author of *7 Daily Choices*

Powerfully written from the eyes of a broken, bruised, and damaged soul due to childhood abuse! Every turn of the page will keep you wondering how God brought this wounded girl through to victory. For anyone who has faced such travesty, or knows of someone who has, Shari Rickenbach's gut-wrenching transparency and compelling story will nudge them towards healing from the vicious soul scars they carry. Through her courageous story, we all begin to understand the severe impact on those victimized by human-trafficking and how to breathe their very soul and life back to them.

-Marian Poeppelmeyer, Trauma and Abuse Recovery Coach & Group Facilitator with the International Institute for Trauma

and Recovery, Author of *Finding My Father – Beyond Tragedy, Through Trauma, and Into Freedom, Road to Freedom Course and Coaching Services*

Echoing Silence from the Child Within is the authentic voice of an adult woman searching to find the sexually abused child she buried in order to survive the horrors of trauma.

-Nanette O'Neal, Transformational Story Coach, Speaker, and Author of the fantasy series *A Doorway Back to Forever*.

The message of *Echoing Silence from the Child Within* is a life-line for the individual who has yet to break their silence due to fear or shame. Shari shows us that it is possible for every person who has been sexually abused to restore their voice and value as they realign to become the person God created them to be. My hope is that those individuals will connect with this book and begin the restoration process. All of creation groans for their manifestation.

-Betty Jewell Slater, Author of *Big Shoes To Fill, How To Establish Your Own Brand When Following In The Footsteps Of An Icon*

Echoing Silence from the Child Within is an amazing book, and Shari's story is important to share in order to help others. She has opened my eyes to the magnitude of sexual abuse in our society today. It really hurts me to realize how many women and men have been sexually abused or molested in just my small circle of acquaintances. Her book is destined to rock the world!

-William Rolling, Confidence Coach and Professional Contractor

Watching the incredible personal work Shari has done to recover from her childhood sexual abuse proves the power of God's healing touch. Shari shows us that every person who has been sexually abused can not only restore their voice and value, but also realign to become the person God created them to be. Shari's powerful message touched my heart as it will yours. If you suffer from sexual abuse, read this story to find hope.

-**Kirsten D Samuel, Author of** *Choosing a Way Out,* **and** *5 Lies Moms Believe,* **Aftershock Recovery Coach**

Echoing Silence from the Child Within

*Restoring Voice and Value
by Rebirthing, Reclaiming, and Realigning
in God's Creative Design*

ECHOING SILENCE FROM THE CHILD WITHIN

Restoring Voice and Value
by Rebirthing, Reclaiming, and Realigning
in God's Creative Design

SHARI RICKENBACH

⅄AUTHOR ACADEMY elite

Printed in the United States of America

Published by Author Academy Elite
PO Box 43
Powell, Ohio 43065

www.authoracademyelite.com

Library of Congress Control Number: 2020923843

Paperback ISBN: 978-1-64746-625-1
Hardcover ISBN: 978-1-64746-626-8
E-book ISBN: 978-1-64746-627-5

Available in hardcover, softcover, e-book, and audiobook.

Scripture quotations taken from the Holy Bible, King James Version

Cover photographs are property of the author Shari Rickenbach

DEDICATION

To my husband, Lee, my rock and strength, whose faithful commitment to love me for better or worse, and whose belief in me held me steady while I worked through childhood trauma and realigned in God's creative design.

ACKNOWLEDGMENTS

Thank you to my coach and mentor Kary Oberbrunner who believed in me when I didn't believe in myself. Your support, encouragement, and always seeing me as transformed gave me the impetus to do the difficult inner work, to go through the pain, and to find the hidden gold, my identity in Christ. I thank God for bringing you into my life to ignite my soul.

Thank you, Daphne Smith, for your stimulating challenges on our weekly coaching calls and holding me accountable. You saw my worth and helped me to find my voice. You have brought out the best in me!

Thanks to Crissy Maier and Bill Rolling, my weekly accountability partners, who were there prodding me on, believing in me that I could finish this book, and for being beta readers. Your input has been valuable to me.

Thank you, Dow Tippet, for your support and creative safe place in the final editing stages of this manuscript. You have given me a priceless gift that I will never forget. And to Saundra S. Rees for your valuable insights in the final line editing.

Thank you, my fellow Fire Ring members, for your weekly support, love, and prayers as I worked through challenging levels of taking *my next best step*. You have stretched me to go beyond my comfort zone.

Thank you to my loving children for giving me space as I worked through things that you did not understand and loved me anyway.

Lee, you have been God's gift to me. You loved me until I could blend back into the one person God created your wife to be. I did the difficult inner work, and you loved me through all the upheaval until I could get there. You are a one-of-a-kind husband, my best friend, confidant, and safe place for 45 years, I am so very blessed to call you mine! I love you.

CONTENTS

FOREWORD

Echoing Silence from the Child Within captures the emotional world of one who is on the journey of restoring voice and value after the trauma of childhood sexual abuse. Shari writes from deep within her heart weaving through her story the ebb and flow of struggling to "come together" after years of living with the shattering effects of abuse.

I feel the pain with her and have watched her struggles. I also sense her triumphs and her incredible tenacity to push through the many and varied obstacles to become a *thriver* and not just a *survivor*.

Do you wonder if it is possible to be free from the patterns of disassociation in order to survive? Shari is honestly raw about the shatteredness that overwhelms victims of traumatic abuse. She has chosen to leave the victim B.E.D, find the O.A.R. of an overcomer, unite with her child within, and now is at peace in her oneness.

Have you lost hope that you will ever restore your own personal voice and value? Follow Shari's principles of *Rebirthing, Reclaiming, and Realigning in God's Creative Design* to discover renewal by bringing every thought into captivity to the mind of Christ. New pathways of thinking can be established, and hope will be ignited by using your power of choice. *Choose life* and you will begin the journey of restoration and lasting transformation.

Over the past three years I have watched her own transformation unfolding as she soars to new heights of life. Her buoyancy and energy are contagious. Her passion to reach out to those who are searching for wholeness from the brokenness of an abusive background will find a compassionate and authentic voice in *Echoing Silence from the Child Within*.

Thank you, Shari, for bravely stepping out into the light of clarity and sharing your journey that others might *Restore Voice and Value* by *Rebirthing, Reclaiming, and Realigning in God's Creative Design*. Her message is destined to ignite souls around the world.

Kary Oberbrunner
CEO of Igniting Souls and author of *Unhackable, Elixir Project, Day Job to Dream Job, The Deeper Path,* and *Your Secret Name*

INTRODUCTION

THE PIT

My silent screams and cries echoed off dark reverberating walls that mocked my soul's longing to find relief and release from the agony of the sexually abused child I had silenced and buried deep within myself. It was a pain of which those closest to me seemed totally unaware.

How does a sexually abused child come to wear the identity of a false self, seemingly effortlessly moving silently from one personality to another? The child's soul reflected the changing seasons of hopes and dreams budding and flowering, but then they faded, withered, and died—and No. One. Noticed. She became like a mirror, reflecting the inner torture of caretakers and adults closest to her. She moved through life as a leaf caught in the current of a mighty river, rushing, crashing, frothing, and foaming. The little leaf is tossed about by powerful forces beyond its control, carried in the grip of movement and power, and like the leaf, the child cannot resist.

This description embodies the emotions that lay buried deep within the soul of a sexually abused child. The warping and distorting of her soul are stored deep in every cell of her body. The nervous system obeys impulses sent in both obvious and subtle body language cues—tones, gestures, looks, words, actions—integrating ambivalent distortions of love/hate, fear/trust, happiness/sadness, guilt/innocence, co-dependence/boundaries, shame/honor, rage/peace. The sexually abused child has no anchor point and knows only what is mirrored to her. She is not emotionally capable of forming her own belief systems, so she absorbs and incorporates negative messages and lives out rigid rules imposed upon her. The innocent child becomes who she is told she is and assumes a false identity to survive. Survival means choosing a lifelong burial of her true self, and burial implies death. It is to live life dead. The choice made so early in life sets in motion the unhealthy behaviors, the habits formed, and the thought patterns that must be changed. The child had no safe person to guide her in these choices and show her a better solution to heal her wounds, so she did the only thing a small child could do to protect herself. She silenced and hid her Inner Child deep within.

That choice came at a high price.

The broken-shattered heart has one source of healing—the adult woman alone must dive deep into her pain to heal herself. She goes alone, because only *she* knows where to find the child hidden deep within. She goes alone, with the purpose to confront, embrace, and release pain. The path this woman travels is cluttered with habits, behaviors, thoughts, and beliefs of others that she absorbed and made hers. Now she has the overwhelming task of years—decades perhaps—to sort through mistaken identity and values to find who she really is. Now, what does the adult woman do with the fear, shame, rage, and guilt that was projected on her? In her searching, she must reach through the deepest pain of the unanswered questions—Who is God to me? —Where was God?—Is God really a God of love?—Does God really love me in all my broken messy?—How can I fix myself so I will be of value and worth?—Who am I?—What is the *truth*?

Why would I even begin to write another story—my story—about abuse? I write because my journey has been long and lonely. I write because searching to find peace in my inner turmoil is what laid the foundation of my faith. This story is what happens when generational abuse occurs. God becomes a distorted image in the child's filter of life. Who is God? Is He really a God of love? If "love" hurts, then why would I want to love a God who hurts children? Is that who He really is? How do I change my filter? If God is love, then why does He allow abuse, evil, and wickedness to exist? How can I trust a God who does not protect an innocent child? Do I really have to love and forgive those who abused me? How?

Perhaps you, too, have asked yourself some hard questions in your life. Maybe you also have been searching for answers to questions that have no answers. What do we do with the perplexities of life that have no answers? How do we fix what is broken inside? How do we remove the pain that eats away at the soul? I believe the solutions for every person are found at the bottom of all that is broken.

We begin to Rebirth what God created perfectly whole, we Reclaim the identity we were created with by finding our identity in Christ, and we Realign our inner core being to God's creative design and begin to co-create with our Creator. In this, we shall have peace. *The Echoing Silence from the Child Within* shall at last find voice and value.

The bedrock of our faith lies in *truth*. It is in the truth of accepting ourselves as broken with no hope of piecing together the billion bits of our messiness. It means embracing all that is broken and hugging all the painful shards that comprise me. It means accepting the truth that being broken has made me who I am. It means I quit running from the shadows of my past. It means acknowledging the fact that I am lovable just as I am, in all my broken messy, the way I am right now. It means I quit lying to myself and embrace the *truth* that there is a God who loves me just as I am, and that He shines through my broken to love the broken. In acceptance lies my peace of mind, body, and soul.

In this peace, I open my heart for you, the reader, to look deep into the soul of a silenced and abused child. The past does not define who we are. Our choices in life set in motion the patterns that are either destructive and keep us locked in pain, or we choose to embrace the pain of change. Gratitude for the gift of pain releases us into the freedom of growth to become who God created us to be. Who am I? is the question that plagues every person who has suffered abuse in any form and to any degree. We have allowed others to define who we are.

In this book I share my own continuing story, an ongoing healing journey of overcoming the shame, rage, guilt, fear, and pain of generational abuse. I am learning how to accept pain as a gift by accepting myself the way God views me as valuable, virtuous, tenacious, and authentic. I am receiving and embracing as my own the names God calls me—undamaged, unbroken, unblemished. I am not just a survivor, but I am an overcoming victor, valued and accepted and loved by the God who is my loving Heavenly Father. I am loved by the God who sees me (Genesis 16:14), and I was loved by the God who saw me when I was exploited.

The purpose of this book is to bring a different perspective to the trauma of soul damage and the destruction left by sexual abuse. As I open my heart to allow the reader to gaze deeply into the wounded soul of an innocent child, I desire to "be the voice" of the millions of children and adolescents who are being ravaged, exploited, and destroyed by the evils of sex trafficking. They have no voice, and they did not choose their plight. They are slaves. They are forced to do the unspeakable against their will. They are bought and sold as merchandise for the gain and pleasure of evil men and women who would dare to violate one of these little ones whom God created for His own purpose and plan to glorify Him.

According to Tim Ballard, founder of Operation Underground Railroad, 200,000 children in the United States alone are slaves of human sex trafficking. (YouTube. Tim Ballard: Operation Underground Railroad, Talks at Google, November 21, 2016.) Now, all estimates point to a considerably higher number in 2020 with the effects of COVID-19 on our culture, and this evil trade has deep roots in the porn industry! Are we a nation that would stoop so low as to sacrifice our children on the altar of pornography and exploit our little ones by selling their bodies and souls for our sexual gratification? The United States is the biggest consumer of child pornography in the world. We do not only want the pictures; we want the child—the innocent little child. Why do we allow such atrocities? Why does the church, this Christian nation, permit this kind of evil to be manifested and acted out on our children? God will not hold us guiltless as a nation, nor will I be guiltless—though I was a victim—if I do not raise my voice to speak for little ones who have no voice or choice.

For those reasons, I have chosen to be open and vulnerable and allow you, the reader, to understand the devastation that occurs deep in the soul of an abused and trafficked child. It is painful and shameful to gaze into the ruin and results of sexual depravity. As a society, we would rather avert our eyes away from soul agony, because to gaze long enough to feel the pain of the helpless child, to feel as Christ feels, to weep as Christ weeps over the ruin of sin, is to enter into the sufferings of Christ. It is so much easier to pretend that the church has no problems buried deep in the hearts of believers. We would rather convince ourselves that salvation will take care of and fix broken people. Our complacency resists involvement. *It's a risky investment of our time and reputation listening to broken and messy.* We choose not to get close to the suffering wounded among us. Perhaps the reason the church cannot love as Christ loves is that sin lies not only at the church door, but it is sitting in the pews and hiding behind the pulpits. Repentance for our sin, as the church, the body of Christ, and as individuals, is the only scriptural remedy!

And so, with my pen as a torch and a beacon of light, I invite you to walk with me into an abyss where there is no light. I welcome your soul to feel, to see, to be touched, and to allow your heart to expand as you listen to the echoing silence buried deep in wounded hearts. I want you to know that in the darkest black abyss is where God Himself leads us to the bottom of our pain, and how He shows us the way through our deepest pain and into Himself, into His heart. He is with us all the way, whether we see or feel Him near. We go alone, but *not alone*. If you will observe and look for Him as you read through *Echoing Silence from the Child Within*, you will see God and know He is your Father, He created you for a purpose, He is Love, He is God, He loves you, He is the Father of lights, and in Him there is no shadow of turning. The abyss is full of light when we co-create with the Father of light.

PART 1
RESTORING VOICE AND VALUE

The ruin of my life was littered with the debris of generational projections of rage, shame, fear, guilt, and pain which I had absorbed and acted out from childhood into adulthood. I open my heart in Part 1 to bring you, the reader, deep into the soul of the sexually abused and exploited child to feel her pain, to watch her struggles, and to walk with her in the depths of a black abyss. You will thereby gain understanding and compassion as she begins her lifelong journey to restore voice and value to herself. The process will differ with every individual, but the basic principles will be the guide. The path to wholeness from the ravages of sexual, physical, emotional, mental, and spiritual trauma is a journey. We find help through counselors, mentors, doctors, and professional therapists who care about us, but we heal and free ourselves from our own self-made prisons. The answers lie deep within and are planted there by the Creator God who made every person in His own image.

1

RECREATING LIFE'S CANVAS

Finding Beauty from Ashes by Accepting *Truth*

The Brand-New Garden Canvas

The soul of a child is like a garden so fair, and Soul Gardens need tender loving care. These gardens grow best when they are nourished in safe, loving environments.

The child's secret Soul Garden was the most exquisite creation she had ever gazed upon. In wonder and delight she flitted from one flower to the next drinking in the heavenly fragrance that filled the air. As a butterfly dances among the flowers in the garden, she danced in childish abandonment to the frequency of who she was created to be. This was her garden. Her Soul Garden. The flowers that grew in abundance had been planted there by the Creator Gardener Himself. She had been created uniquely. No other person on earth knew the hidden beauty waiting to burst forth and bless the world with the fragrance of her life lived in full bloom. Her soul was tuned to sing the frequency of the song God had created in her—her song, the song of who she is in the moment, and His song to be lived out to the fullest of her potential while co-creating His story written in her.

This secret Soul Garden was the place where her identity was to be nurtured and guarded with jealous care. The fountain of joy bubbling up in the midst of the garden was tapped into the source of Life that flowed straight from the heart of God. Love ever new filled her Soul Garden with sunshine and light that reflected the beauty hidden within. Day by day God was painting the canvas of her life in the vibrant beauty of the flowers of tranquility, gentleness, kindness, faith, belief, hope, patience, goodness, quietness, sweetness, delight, and trust, and vivacious bubbly tenacity anchored the root system of the essence of who she was created to be in the Creator Gardener Himself.

There were intriguing little paths that wound through her Soul Garden leading to undiscovered nooks of flowers waiting to be explored. What was just around the next bend? Adventure, curiosity, wonderment, creativity, and imagination were flowers that popped out in the most unexpected places bringing beaming smiles of joy as she danced her way on to the next hidden arbor.

The rosebushes of passion and purpose, generosity and gratitude, compassion and calmness were loaded with tender buds forming delicate little promises of beauty to come. The Gardener also planted certain seeds deep within her being that she would discover much later as she carefully cultivated and watered her rose gardens. These were plants that needed years of hidden growth to develop the roots reaching deep into her core being to anchor her in authenticity, commitment, courage, adaptability, resilience, passionate perseverance, faithfulness, and integrity.

In the inner secret sanctuary of her garden, the Creator Gardener had carefully planted the flowers of innocence and purity. He had built a special walled fence of protection all around these two flowers and gave great attention to the nurturing and growth process. And, with great skill, the Creator of life safely concealed the entrance gate with His plan that she would present her most treasured gift of virtue to her husband at the marriage altar as she promised to love and to cherish him until death parted them. She was just a child, but this was the Master Creator Gardener's future plan for her.

Intertwined among the most treasured and fragrant flowers of innocence and purity, there was one flower of delicate beauty that was going to require diligent watchful care, nourishment, and careful cultivation in the formative years. This little flower bud was designed by God to produce the most gorgeous and exquisitely sensitive flower ever created. This was the flower Gift of Virtue. This was the flower that rooted the child in the essence of who she was created to be. Every other flower and the unique fragrance of each flower drew nourishment from this deep inner hidden source of life. This flower of virtue was connected to the heart of God who is the Creator Gardener.

The Secret Soul Garden was growing more beautiful with each passing day. Her sunshiny exuberance for life filled the garden with joyous laughter and she sang from early morning until her sleepy eyes closed at night. As flowers that bloom in the Spring bring newness of life and bright happy colors opening to the warmth of the sunshine, so was her Soul Garden bursting with potential to bless the world with the fragrance of her life lived in full bloom. The flowers of truthfulness and trust grew closely together in bright yellow clumps. Each flower was delicately painted with crimson centers from which intricate tiny crimson veins flowed up into the ruffled creamy yellow tips of the petals. Entangled throughout the masses of yellow and crimson the Creator Gardener had planted the seeds of His Love. The blooms on all the flowers of His Love presented indescribable beauty of refracted light that gave a transparent glow from the center of her inner being. These were her favorite flowers. She was who He had created her to be.

You have been looking into the original creation of the Soul Garden of a small child. This is a true story. This child I am talking about is a *real* child. She and I have much to tell you.

The Soul Garden had a darling picket fence that was just high enough to keep out unwanted beasts of prey, and the inner beauty of her garden pulsated with so much joy and light that predators drew back. However, there was something within the soul of this vulnerable child that these beasts smelled and desired. She was trusting. She believed whatever she was told. Trust was her favorite flower. It matched exactly how she felt inside her Soul Garden—her heart full of sunshiny radiance pulsating with love that flowed from the heart of God. What was there not to trust? She had a heart full of love for everybody and knew no stranger. To her, the whole world was just like she was. She saw no differences of skin color, hair color, eye color, short, tall, boy, girl, man, or woman—all people were the same to be loved the same. And because she loved with the love of the Creator Gardener's Love, she believed that all people in the world had the same kind of love.

Giving and *Sharing* were two other gorgeous flowers growing in lovely vines, climbing up over the picket fence and spilling their loads of fragrant blossoms into the street for anyone passing by to gather armloads of radiant joy. Comforted and cheered, they walked away with hope ignited in hearts that had been heavy with the cares of life. How was it that a little child's Soul Garden could have such impact on others?

How was it that beasts of prey would be so hardened that they wanted to trample the beauty within the soul of a child? These beasts began their grooming process by lurking and watching for moments when they could be alone and draw the child into conversation. They told her they loved her flowers. They asked if she would share some of the flowers blooming inside of her garden. Oh, yes, they liked the ones hanging over the fence, but the flowers they wanted, she would need to pick and make a special bouquet just for them. These bouquets would be special secrets that she shared only with them. Would she just please open the gate a little bit so they could really see all of her flowers?

Those scary beasts were at her gate again! Heart thumping hard in her chest, she drew away from the evil glint in their eyes and turning, she ran as fast as her little legs could carry her to the safety of the inner secret sanctuary deep within her Soul Garden. Shaking in fear, she gently touched her little quivering lips to her flowers of innocence and purity while hugging the flower Gift of Virtue close as she whispered, "My beautiful flowers! I'm so afraid! Somehow, I know you are all in danger, but I don't know how to protect you! The beasts are too big! Are they going to break down the walls and destroy the gate and come into to steal you away from me?"

Huddling in a corner of her sanctuary—she waited, listening as footsteps faded away and the vulgar raucous laughter sounded far away. Creeping forth from her hiding place, she tiptoed all through her Soul Garden inspecting each dainty flower that made up the essence of who she was. They hadn't gotten in. All of the flowers looked shaken though, as if an earthquake tremor had moved through her Soul Garden. She picked up her flowers--*Compassion* and *Sensitivity*, then adding *Brave* and *Caring* to her heart bouquet, she knelt beside all the flowers in her Soul Garden and comforted them until they felt safely anchored in the soil of her heart again.

3:00 a.m.

I jolted awake with two searing words screaming and demanding my attention like neon lights blinking from the dark recesses of my emotional being. SHAME. CODEPENDENCY.

Oh! Please, not *that*! Shame like scalding hot waves swept through my body as I lay staring into the darkness of my bedroom. Why *this*? Why *now*? Why was this inner heat burning and igniting the fortified fortress of my "good girl" façade? Days turned to weeks as the hot waves turned into living flames leaping forward like a raging fire devouring and consuming acres of lush forest surrounding my fortress to feed its insatiable hunger. Shame burned its way through every cell of my body. For weeks, shame burned and devoured every barrier I had neatly built throughout my life as protection.

All I could see was charred and smoking ruins, devastation, and destruction. Beauty from ashes? Could there be life after death?

Yes. This is what the path of healing looks like—pain that devours the woundedness and leaves the abused soul with nothing good or beautiful, only stark, naked *truth*. What is left is the real me, the result of abuse. Here is where I start with nothing but ashes, nothing good to offer God.

And...God...Smiled.

God smiled because He saw that I was now ready for Him to begin recreating good from chaos and soul destruction. God saw beauty for ashes. In that burning, the refuse of life is consumed. The landscape is laid naked and bare in all its ugliness and charred ruin. Yet strangely, new life is stirring within the soul of the sexually abused. What looks like total ruin and death to the eye of the beholder is really the kiss of life. Life has been breathed into the child's shattered soul. The breath of God breathes creative newness into the soul scarred by abuse. And hidden beauty springs forth. New life? New beginnings? Yes! The child she buried within can live!

The seeds that God Himself planted in her soul, the essence and fragrance of who she really is—the one He created—never dies and is never destroyed. No wrong done to an innocent child can destroy God's own creation because that soul will live forever—because God is Good. The results of sin and the generational effects of sin do not change who God is or that He is Good.

The mind, body, and soul of the child born into circumstances beyond her control cannot fathom the goodness of a God who seems to look the other way ignoring her pain, shame, guilt, fear, and rage. The little child begins to form false belief systems. From this foundation, she fabricates and embraces a false self to protect her identity, because her inner child, the real and true person she is, must be protected at all costs.

And so, the perfect and whole person God created, the soul who had His smile of approval because He knew His creation was good, goes into hiding. She hides deep within, and God saw her.

And...God...Saw...Her.

The churning emotions buried deep within the silenced child echo from the dark abyss of her soul, demanding to be recognized for what they are—damaged emotions. The years have wreaked havoc, and now her inner being is a huge, tangled ball of broken chaos. It is the filter that all life has flowed through. Perfection in chaos? Be good enough? How?

Both the church and the world look on and say—*Not beautiful—we like beautiful people.*

Too messy—not my problem.

Just get your act together. Just move on. Get on with life.

Really? That's how to love broken humanity? "Love" was distorted in the long-ago forever moments, and now you would tell the sexually abused soul she just needs to forgive and forget as if the tangled mess of her life is miraculously and instantly a living tapestry of exquisite beauty?

In the murky abyss of her soul, she wanders through life, searching for herself, not knowing who she is. Her soul is shattered and every piece of herself she finds she compares to "good enough." She is never able to measure up to what is displayed as the highest good while being made to live out the sordid and evil as good. What child can discern who is safe? Or who can be trusted? She has no sense of her beginning and does not know her ending. She has no concept of boundaries, no knowledge that personal space is to be honored, respected, and regarded as her sacred right. She only knows compliance to whims of others to use her and then cast her on the dunghill of refuse and be told she is no good, a liar and such a bad person that nobody will ever love her.

The child is cut adrift with no inner stability deep in the mind where the emotional conflicts rage. How did she get here? She does not know. Her mind fiercely blocks what every cell in her body has stored away of horrendous memories. They are lodged there waiting until the Child Within gets her attention through pain. It does not matter whether her internal pain speaks from the physical, emotional, mental, or spiritual realms. She has only one consuming instinct—to preserve and fight for her very existence just to survive from one day to the next.

Mental, physical, emotional, social, spiritual, sensory, sexual, and creative health is impaired from the start of her life. The child forced into adult roles is so shattered and broken within, yet she is required to wear the mask of a false identity and function as if life is normal and beautiful. Except she has no clue what is healthy or beautiful. She only knows what is normal for her.

She is set into patterns and choices of behavior at such an impressionable age that she loses complete touch with who she is, but the miracle of our Creator God—who has planted the essence of who she is—speaks from the grave. The soul of the child is restless. She wants to live—fully live life in *full* bloom. She wants to create. She wants to thrive. She wants to laugh, to sing, to dance, to cry, to *Be*. She knocks from deep within and waits for the false self to step aside and let her live the full essence of who she was created to be. She wants to bless the world with the fragrance of her life lived in full bloom.

Why does she wait for someone outside of herself to provide refreshing healing waters to quench her soul thirst? Because she is growing up in a dysfunctional codependent home. She knows nothing else. She has no internal moorings. The deep internal struggle for existence begins. It is an internal war that goes on for what seems an eternity. Why?

She is looking outside of herself for answers, not knowing that the answers are hidden within. Her healing lies dormant deep inside her cells. The person God created her to be peeks out every now and then. She is vivacious, saucy, spirited, tenacious, fun-loving, caring, compassionate, gentle, kind, a truth-teller, and a bundle of sunshine. Dysfunctional family members do not care to see that side of her. She is too free. She is like a bird on wing flying higher than their grasping reach as they try to pull her back, smother her, and cram her into the boxy vault they made for her. They want to control her and rob her of her God-given identity.

Life stirs from deep within. Life speaks from the depths of the silent echoing cries of her soul. Restless waves like birthing contractions propel her forward to the light. Her spirit is reaching, reaching for the light. She was never made to live in dark despair. She was not created for this.

Smothering shame. Tides of guilt. Projected currents of rage that grab her soul and pull and drag her to icy frozen depths. Isolated in her grief and pain, she guards her true self in fierce control by building inward walls of perfection. She is working, working—always working—*never* stopping to rest, restore, rejuvenate, or reclaim her creative beauty. She thinks she will find goodness and wholeness in doing and perfecting the ruin of her soul.

But what is *truth*? Where is compassion? Where is God in all that appears to be the opposite of *truth*? Can there be release from her pain? How is it that perpetrators can inflict such atrocities upon a child and society shelters them while the child bears the shame of their evil deeds? She is told she is a liar and *never* tells the truth. How does she believe and trust in a God who never seems to be there for her? Is she justified in embracing the distortions of who God seems to be? If God made her, cares about her, loves her, and says His values are to be her highest *truth*, how does she attain such lofty perspectives? Her questions always return to *Who am I? Where was God?*—This is the sad refrain that grooves the thought patterns deep in her brain and that fuels her soul distress.

She doubts the reality of a loving God. She allows the doubts to fragment further her already shattered soul. Abuse shakes apart the very foundations of the soul and leaves her empty and dry. She is thirsting for living water to quench her yearning soul. She avoids the place of her healing.

Why? Because she cannot grasp the fact that at the bottom of her dark abyss is the answer to the *truth* she desperately seeks. The abyss is her scary hard. Because if she goes to the bottom of her abyss, she will have to confront the rage she has embraced and then blamed God for the silenced buried child she locked away. She wants freedom, but freedom comes with a huge price tag. The price is humility in asking the God she hates to forgive her. She needs forgiveness for projecting the actions of wicked, evil men and the neglect of parental love and nurturing to be equal with who God is. In the distorting and fragmenting, she places the blame on God as if He were the one who sought to destroy her soul.

She wants to be valued for who she was created to be, and yet she rejects the person God created as not "good enough." What does she really want? The *truth* deep inside. The *truth* that sets her soul free. How does she gain her freedom? In acceptance. In *acceptance*? You mean she only needs to choose *truth*? Freedom is a choice? Only a *choice*? There is nothing she must do or work out?

God made her, and His values are her highest *truth*. In the acceptance of *truth*, she has given herself value because His *truth* is her *truth*. In acceptance of *truth* she is set free. Her prison doors open to life—life that is abundant. She has hope as she leaves her self-righteous robes of hopeless denial of truth behind. The insidious sin of sexual abuse is that the victim projects all her fear, shame, blame, guilt, and pain on God. Yes, she was a victim of horrendous atrocities, but the God who created her did not create sin or inflict her damaged soul with this kind of pain. God does not do that to His own creations. Man, in his fallen nature, is the one who acts out the wickedness of his own heart. Doubting a loving God and equating Him with sinful men was her insidious sin that she confessed to God and for which she asked His forgiveness. The *truth* is her healing foundation for wholeness of mind, body, and soul.

In acceptance of *truth*, she begins her long journey to wholeness by opening her heart to the possibilities of change by making hard choices. She chooses to acknowledge she buried the person God created her to be deep inside of her as her only recourse for survival. She was the one who silenced the inner child and shut her up in a very dark abyss. She chose to separate the child from her body, and only she could go to where the child had been waiting and knocking on her inner being for more than sixty years, asking for freedom of mind, body, and soul.

Her birth names mean *princess* and *refreshing one*, but *liar, invisible, enslaved, rejected, unwanted, alone, powerless, fat thing, good girl—control girl* were her given names. Dare she step into that dark and scary abyss? How will she bring all those other personalities of given names together when she is so fragmented? Who is she really? Beauty from ashes?

Her life's canvas was ruined. How does she fix it? She *cannot* fix it. She must embrace *truth* and give the brush of her life to the Master Artist, who is Christ Himself. She is not blotted out of the picture of her life. The Master Artist knows her, and He begins mixing new colors to transform the ruined details of her life and weave her story into a canvas of exquisite beauty that shines with His love and His handiwork. He transforms the *ashes* of life into *beauty*. His transformations in her happen only by her choice to accept and embrace *truth*.

In this she will find worth and value, as we shall soon see when she recognizes the need to value herself as God values her. Her worth is more than a jar of pennies!

2

RECOGNIZING THE NEED TO VALUE MYSELF AS GOD VALUES ME

Reaffirming *Truth* by Accepting My Worth

The small suitcase was packed, ready for an exciting adventure with someone she loved and trusted. Tucking her favorite baby doll under her arm with the demeanor of a princess, she confidently ran to the car awaiting her departure. Her doll clasped in a tight embrace, her little suitcase in the other hand, in joyous anticipation of the journey ahead, she paused at the open car door for one last picture—innocence shining from her pure soul. She was three years old.

This journey would be the end of carefree childhood and the beginning of her lifelong journey searching for the person God created her to be.

The Child's Secret Soul Garden

Tired from all the excitement of the day and the extra work in her Soul Garden, she fell into a deep sleep. Was she dreaming? Something strange was happening! There was a different kind of beast beside her. Somehow it had come to her Soul Garden and was stealing her flower of innocence while she was sleeping! She was frozen in fear! Waking from the nightmare, her body convulsing in sobs, she felt the beast press a shiny copper penny into each small fist.

Alone, confused, terrified, the child lay staring into the darkness, her soul burning with a sense and awareness something shameful had just occurred. It made her stomach twist into a tight knot. Why had a beast been in her bed? Why did she wake up and find there was a shiny penny in each little fist? She had been asleep. Was this a bad dream? What was going to happen tomorrow? She was going to spend the day at a house very close to where she remembered more beasts lived, and she was going to spend the night in that same house! How was she going to protect her Soul Garden now that the gate had a broken latch? She didn't know how the latch had broken while she was asleep, and now she couldn't find anything to fix it with. It was so dark and scary all of a sudden.

Morning came at last, but inside her Soul Garden there was a strange foggy cloud that had created a weird looking plant of fearfulness that was taking root very quickly threatening to overspread the whole garden. Everything looked different this morning, and she noticed there were wide gaps in the picket fence all around her Soul Garden. Strangely quiet, the child sat beside her flower of innocence. It lay broken and mangled in the soil of her heart. She had no name, no words to describe this cloud that had descended over her garden. It was like a shroud that left her defenseless. Shame was the name, but she was too small to know this feeling had a name.

Breakfast didn't taste good and tears choked her until she couldn't swallow. Pushing away from the table, she slowly picked up her baby doll hugging it closely, the tears streaming down her cheeks. It was time to go to the other house. Why did she feel so scared? Her heart garden had been so full of light the night before, and she had been jumping for joy in anticipation of tomorrow. Now, the ugly weeds of dread and fear grew quickly into big, tangled knots throughout her Soul Garden as she climbed into the car for the ride to where she would be staying.

The ride ended too soon. Hugging her doll tightly, the child walked slowly toward the house glancing fearfully over her shoulder to see if the beasts were waiting behind the bushes and trees. Seeing nothing, she breathed a sigh of relief and ran into the open arms of someone at the doorway. Sobbing out her heart she buried her face in the comforting apron that smelled like fresh bread and snuggled into the warm arms holding her close. Exhausted from the terror of the night and spent from crying, the squeaking rocker lulled her into deep sleep.

And as she slept, two beasts of prey entered the house. Noticing the small figure sleeping on the couch, they asked how long she was going to be there. Pretending concern and care for the little one, they offered to help watch her when she woke up. They would make sure she would be safe if she wanted to play with them outdoors before supper. It would work best for everybody, especially with company coming—and she was always wanting to be in the kitchen "helping"—but actually being a nuisance with her nonstop questions and getting in the way.

Giving each other a sly wink, the beasts left the house and went about the day as usual. Gleefully, they secretly planned the fun they were going to have before supper. It would be even more fun since others would be there too.

The child awoke, and sitting up, looked fearfully around the room. There was that certain smell of the beasts still lingering in the air. Where were they? Jumping up, she ran to the kitchen looking for safety.

A smiling face greeted her, and her fears subsided as she climbed up on the lap waiting to hold her. Cookies and milk always tasted better there. Munching the yummy goodness, she was oblivious to the tears streaming down the cheeks of the one holding her.

How could she know that another child, the same size, had at one time, also, sat on the same lap eating *her* cookies. That other child, who had been but a child herself, had died while birthing a child. This child, sitting on the same lap many years later, had no knowledge of the deep grief that gripped a mother's sorrowing heart for *her* innocent child who had been destroyed because of generational abuse. Knowing it was her responsibility to protect this little one in her arms, but unable, she sat frozen in her own grief. Buried emotions of grief overwhelmed her, and a strange numbness clouded her mind. The incessant chatter of the child sitting on her lap flowed over her tired mind and body and soul increasing the numbness she felt.

It was getting late in the afternoon and company was coming. She would send the child outdoors for a few minutes of playtime on the porch where she would be safe.

The company beasts had arrived sooner than expected and were waiting for this moment. Enticing the child with promises of very special secret flowers they wanted to show her, they told her to leave her baby doll on the porch and come play with them. She wouldn't need the baby doll, and it was going to be so fun to play this new game. This game would be all about her flowers, and they had new secret flowers they wanted to plant in her garden. She was going to love these flowers because they were very different than hers.

She didn't like these beasts, but they were the same ones she saw at church and other places where her family visited. They had come to her house too. The beasts had never wanted to play with her before, so she wondered why they needed her flowers to play a new secret game.

She had never used her flowers to play a game. She did love flowers. She loved to look at all kinds of flowers, loved to touch the soft petals, and loved to bury her nose in the delightful fragrance of every flower she saw.

And they had said that they just *knew* she was going to love to touch and smell the secret flowers. Maybe, she would go see the secret flowers for a minute and then run back to the porch. But how did they know she had flowers in her Soul Garden? Would these new flowers help fix her flower of innocence that got ruined last night? These were smaller beasts, but maybe they weren't like that different kind of beast. They seemed to really love her flower gardens and wanted to help her plant more flowers.

She didn't know what secret flowers looked like. How could she get some of these flowers to plant? Maybe, she could plant these flowers in front of the gate to her garden, and they would grow high enough to cover the broken latch. She didn't want any of the beasts to know that the lock had somehow been broken last night. She was so afraid the big beasts of prey were going to see the broken latch and take the gate right off the hinges! Her picket fence was already wobbly, and her garden didn't feel safe. No! She would not go with the small beasts to play their flower game! She turned and ran inside the house!

Where do you find innocence when childhood is stolen? What value, what worth can you place on stolen innocence if it can never be restored?

Pennies. A small fistful of shiny copper *Pennies.* Was that all her soul was worth? *Pennies* traded for innocence.

She did *not* like pennies. Pennies made her cry and feel afraid. She ran away as fast as her little legs could carry her when she saw pennies, but longer bigger legs ran faster and brought her back. She did *not* like the secrets she got pennies for. They were *not* nice secrets and she felt so dirty. Why did God *not* help her? Maybe she was *not* good enough. Pennies

17

weren't very much money. Maybe she was *not* worth even a penny. Maybe that's why God never helped her. Maybe God could *not* see her in that dark building. Maybe God did *not* love bad dirty little girls.

And so, the child's value system became rooted in twisted and distorted realities. Core beliefs can never find stability in a faulty shaking foundation. Core beliefs must be grounded and anchored in truth; now, she was cut adrift from the internal emotional stability which she should have absorbed in the ebb and flow of life lived in a safe environment.

Where was safety? Who could she trust? Why was her truthful story a lie? Why did family members call her *Liar* and look at her with anger? *Liar* was a hurtful ugly name, and she wondered if her birth name with the meaning, a Princess, was really her own name anymore. She did *not* feel loved like she had been before she went on that journey. She began to be afraid of everyone and everything. She not only *felt* dirty, ugly, and bad—She *was* dirty. She *was* ugly. She *was* bad.

Who was she supposed to be? Was she just a toy doll to be used up and tossed in the trash? What was happening to her? Why didn't she feel happy and safe? Why did she always have to be on guard and running away from people who said they loved her? Where could she find a safe place to hide? Her bedroom was not safe. Outdoors was not safe. The barn was not safe.

Maybe if she could just crawl inside herself then no one could find her and hurt her again. That was it! The perfect hiding place was deep inside herself! No one could find her! No one could hurt her! She was *NOT* her body! Her body was the Liar, the Dirty One, the Bad Girl, the Ugly Thing, the Fat Thing! Those names did not belong to her. And her body did not belong to her. Bad things were happening to her body, but not to *her*. Yes, the only safe place in her world was deep inside herself, away from her body.

This was the best secret hiding place ever! Now she knew exactly what to do! When there was no safe place that she could run to, she would hide inside herself allowing only her body to be hurt! She knew how to separate her body from herself. They could not hurt *her* anymore. And she did *not* have room for pennies in *her* secret hiding place. Pennies were for her *body*. Not for *her*. Pennies did not belong to *her*. Pennies could not hurt *her*.

But why did people give pennies for her body? Was she like a penny? Was she worth only a penny? Does God think bad, dirty, ugly little girls are worth only a penny? She wonders why, if God made her, why is her worth equal to a penny? Does God care about what is happening? Can He *not* see when people are hurting her? Why won't God protect her? Does He like to see her pain, her soul agony? Why does God leave her alone? Is God deaf, so He cannot hear her cries for help? What did she do to make God so mad at her? Does God hate her like some people hate her?

The child's emotional, mental, spiritual, and physical anguish increases with every passing year. She begins to reason within herself that God will never love her unless she is good enough. She arrives at the conclusion that God does not care about her—She is not good enough for Him to love and protect her—God does not protect her—so she will protect herself—*deep inside herself.*

The *Good Enough Girl* was the name of the first thick wall of protection she built around her heart. Safety. No one could hurt her. No one would find out her heart was wounded, bleeding, broken, shattered. The *Good Enough Girl* had an identical twin sister, the *Good Girl,* who was working frantically to put up the next barrier—she *had* to build it *perfect.* No one would see the shattered messy broken inside her heart because she would take all the pieces and remake them into something *perfect and beautiful.* Then the *Control Girl* joined in, working day and night slathering on the internal emotional mortar that was harder than any granite stone. She would make sure she was never out of control ever again! The *Invisible Girl* wove her transparent web delicately and intricately by entirely enclosing her hiding place with tendrils that anchored themselves in every part of her emotional being. Now, if life was too hard, she could easily detach herself from her body. When her place of refuge was ready, the *Silent Girl* walked in, closed, locked, and threw away the key to the door of her heart. Smothering darkness gripped her soul, she screamed in terror—only to hear *echoing silence.*

Silence—*Echoing Silence.* The place she thought was her safety was now her prison—

The false identity that the sexually abused child wears is just a mask. She takes on the names given to her, acts them out, making them her own. Each time she accepts projected rage, guilt, shame, blame, or pain from an adult and acts out what is not hers to own—she experiences soul fracturing. For many victims of sexual abuse, the only way to survive is to disassociate. The internal earthquake produced using this means of survival shatters and pulverizes the already fragmented soul. The mind cannot hold the horror of atrocities being inflicted upon the body.

The child needs an anchor in her chaos, so when she discovers how to remove herself from the pain by choosing to disassociate, she chooses what became for her a type of addiction. She chooses to stay stuck in her self-made prison because panic drives her to the only place of safety she can find—it is not safety.

Dissociating is her only means of survival. This choice silences the Child Within, and her growth emotionally and socially is greatly stunted. In fact, her emotional growth stops where the trauma began unless help is quickly found for her. She has chosen the silence because she lives in fear. Outwardly she manages to function as any growing child, but what is happening within is the flight, fight, and/or freeze modes which are being reinforced daily. Extreme energy is expended, and she is left exhausted physically, mentally, spiritually, and emotionally.

She has great difficulty focusing on her schoolwork. She is irritable and irrational at times and those around her do not understand. Those closest to her, whether they be her teachers, parents, siblings, or friends, do not understand her. Some do not try to understand or want to understand her emotional distress. Rather, her distress is amplified as she becomes the *Invisible One*. The child is pushed aside, expected to carry out responsibilities that are far beyond her capabilities, and she is treated as if she were an adult.

As I tell you this child's story, my story, I am speaking from the depths of the inner pit where I lived for many years. The details of names, places, and specifics are missing because your story is not my story. I no longer live in that pit. You do not have to live in a pit of dark despair either.

As you continue to walk with me though each chapter, I am pointing you, the reader, to where I found how to give myself voice and value. Healing from abuse takes time. The silenced and abused child who lived in me for decades was crying for release from her prison of pain. I locked her up and threw away the key to deliverance from emotional, sexual, spiritual, physical, and verbal abuse. My story includes and addresses the painful issues of generational abuse as well.

Each generation has the choice to change their own behaviors and refuse to be the victims of the past. We choose to change our stories. We choose to be the authors of change. We choose to get out of the victim B.E.D. of *blame, excuses,* and *denial.* I chose to burn my victim B.E.D.; I chose to pick up my O.A.R. by taking *ownership,* being *accountable,* and taking *responsibility* for everything in my life that transpired from the results of my own decisions.

We will examine these concepts deeper, a little further on our journey, but credit belongs to Kary Oberbrunner for his insights and teachings with these two concepts of B.E.D. and O.A.R. I read, reread, absorbed, and assimilated two of Kary's books which describe these concepts in *Your Secret Name* and *The Deeper Path.* The path of healing is different for every person simply because God did not create any of us from the same mold. However, the concepts and principles we glean from other authors and professionals who point us to helps and tools for our journeys are people we thank God for and bless. They cared enough to reach out and offer help when we were drowning in our despair.

Humility is action in full motion when we, as abuse victims, receive and accept the fact that I am not responsible for what happened to me, but I am responsible for what I do with who I am as a person. Abuse is humiliating and leaves us shrouded in shame that does not belong to us. As victims we somehow take responsibility for what occurred. *Receiving* and *accepting* the truth that I am *not* responsible for the actions of another person is the action of humility. *Humility is what transforms humiliation into the perpetual motion of opening the door to freedom.* And freedom is my choice.

Humility then becomes the beautiful garment of Grace that we choose to clothe ourselves with every moment of every day. I either choose to wear the shame forced upon me, or I choose to wear the beauty of humility. *Choosing is perpetual motion.* Abuse does not define us or identify us. We are not *abuse.* Perpetrators can never take away our power of choice. God created us with free will and the power of choice. Choice is my gift to embrace. *We are created by God for a purpose, and no one can destroy who God created us to BE.*

No abuser, no type of abuse, or degree of abuse can destroy who I am—my identity can never be destroyed. I am a soul created by God. My soul and your soul will live forever.

And so, this brings us to the thought of value and worth. If I as a person was valued at one penny—one cent—one shiny copper penny—how do I change my thoughts and mindsets that channel and funnel all thought processes subconsciously through a filter that is clogged with false concepts and belief systems?

Truth is my value—my worth. The truth is that God created me and knew me before I was born. He made me unique. There is only one me. This is the same for every person on the planet. God made every single person an individual who is totally unique. When we try to be someone else and fit a mold other than who God created us to be, we lose our creative uniqueness that we were designed with. We forfeit our purpose for why God created us in the first place.

I have a unique purpose and a gift in me to give to this world that no one else has. I have a reason to live life to the fullest of my potential. I may not see my gift if I see only negativity and chaos in a filter clogged with false concepts. Our filters do not need to stay clogged. We are not doomed to be victims of sexual abuse, or victims of any kind of abuse! We have a beautiful golden key to life abundant and a life lived in rich delight knowing who we are in Christ.

The golden key to life abundant is found when we bring our thoughts into captivity! My thoughts were what kept me locked up in a deep and extremely dark pit. My thoughts kept me silenced and isolated because I lived in constant fear. God did not create any human being to live life in fear. We were created to live life in harmony and love. The mind, body, and spirit work together when every thought is brought into captivity. This is the simple power of choice. I have this power of choice in me until the day I die. What will I choose? Peace or Panic?—My brain is not designed to have both. Faith or Fear?—My heart is not designed for both. Trust or Torment?—My spirit is not designed for both.

The choice to embrace painful memories *and* the emotions that were attached to those memories was the turning point in my healing journey. God took time teaching me that my value is much more than one shiny copper penny. My Creator had a surprise waiting for me in a gallon jar full of pennies, nickels, dimes, and quarters.

God cared about every detail in my life so much that He had my husband clean out his pockets nightly and deposit the small change into this old jar. A simple act that became a daily habit. A habit that was to become my future blessing and gift. This gift was the golden key I used to begin turning the rusty corroded lock of my prison—the prison of toxic fear and negative thoughts!

God cares about the smallest details of our lives and uses the simple everyday happenings which seem so insignificant to reveal to us that He was there all the time. A jar of old coins would be incredibly significant as I will describe to you later how I used the pennies to organize, represent, and divide my entire life into time periods.

3

RECONCILING TO GOD BY EMBRACING PAIN

Grieving the Losses of Childhood

The Child's Secret Soul Garden (continued)

Disappointed that their plan hadn't worked, the smaller beasts went to talk to the bigger beasts. Remembering the child had left her baby doll on the porch, one of them ran to snatch it up and hid it in a bush near a shed. Talking together, the big and small beasts planned to wait until after supper when everyone was busy, and they would use the doll to entice the child to go look for it. Then, they would all play the flower game together with her. Oh! Don't forget the pennies! Make sure you all have a pocket full of bright shiny pennies ready for her! She'll get a penny for each time she touches and smells the secret flowers! She's going to love our flowers!

The vulgar raucous laughter drifted through the open kitchen window, and the child heard. Shrinking back into the corner, she hid behind the cold wood stove shaking in fright.

The laughter drew nearer, and then she heard the steps of heavy boots clumping across the porch. The screen door slammed behind them, and their loud voices filled the small kitchen demanding their food to be dished up right away. They had important work to get finished before dark. The beasts had taken over the kitchen. The small and the big.

She curled into a tight little ball behind the stove her heart pounding in fear. The knot in her stomach moved into her throat. She was choking. And sensing a movement above her, she felt a smothering icy wave of terror sweep through her body. A hand was reaching for her.

The beasts had found her! An icy black wave swept over her, numbing her senses as the hand lifted the small body by one arm from her hiding place. Blackness engulfed the child's Soul Garden as she was carried into the shed.

Secret flowers? They weren't showing her flowers like she had in her gardens. Her gardens were full of light and colorful beauty.

This wasn't a flower game. There were no flowers in the shed. Passed from beast to beast as a toy, they played their flower game—It wasn't a game. There were no flowers—

They gave her shiny copper pennies. As the pile of pennies grew—her Soul Flowers died one by one.

God knew He had created me to be a creative visual person. He knew how to bring me to the point where I was ready to set myself free from the prison I had created in childhood. Remember, I thought I had found a place of safety by dissociating. No safety there. I had locked myself away with fearful negative thought patterns. How could I ever free myself? God was going to use pennies!

I moved the jar of pennies in my husband's office every time I vacuumed the carpet. I moved it every week for years and never saw *pennies*. Then one day I began to be uneasy every time I noticed the jar. Uneasiness began to stir emotions that I had stuffed and denied. I did not like the feeling that grabbed my stomach and the way my heart would squeeze in dread. *Pennies.* What was this? I tried to push it all aside. My body began speaking louder when I did not listen to the whispers from my heart. Weird terrifying dreams plagued me disrupting sleep patterns. Days turned into weeks, then months, then years.

Pennies. What was speaking from the grave where I had buried my inner child by refusing to listen to her cries for freedom? What was this restlessness that gripped me, leaving me with consuming fear? Why did I see a jar of screws while I was washing dishes, and suddenly break out in a cold sweat, my heart pounding in terror? Memories.

Memories that I had locked away until I, the adult woman, could allow myself to feel the pain and emotions of the helpless child who was sexually abused. I was an adult, but fear of the past kept me bound. I had no idea that freedom was a choice away. The simple choice my husband made to save loose change in a gallon jar was soon to be the golden key I would pick up to unlock the door to painful buried memories. Memories my body, mind, and soul could no longer hold. Secrets too shameful to look at.

I had to *Look. Acknowledge. Confront. Embrace. Feel. Experience. Grieve.*

Then *celebrate* that I could choose *Life*—choosing to bring my thoughts into captivity. My healing journey would take a turn around in the right direction at this point.

The Jar of Pennies

I woke up one morning with the thought that I needed to go get the jar of pennies. How weird. It made me feel uneasy and uncomfortable. Why should I go get the jar of pennies? Why was

I so afraid? The more I thought about the jar of pennies I was gripped with terror. Weird.

Pennies do not have power. Or do they? Why do I not want to look? Look where? Oh! That abyss! Pennies have something to do with the abyss and I am frozen in fear! Do I dare look into the darkness of the abyss? What is this panic that is squeezing the air from my lungs? Why am I frantically running away inside of me, but frozen in fear? What am I supposed to do with this fear? What will happen to me if I walk down the hallway to my husband's office and pick up the jar of pennies? Am I going to get hurt again? Absurd! How will a jar of pennies hurt me?

The jar and the contents are not the problem—I have deep emotional issues that are speaking in loud clear tones demanding my attention. Choice. This is the day! Today I choose freedom!

I choose to pick up the jar—my hands are shaking, cold and clammy. My heart is pounding so hard it feels like my chest will explode. I carry the jar thrust away from my body back to my studio and gingerly place it on the table. My legs are quivering as I collapse into a chair. I sit staring at the jar—my whole inner being recoiling in fear as if I had just placed in front of me a rattlesnake, coiled, ready to strike.

Memories. Emotions attached to every memory. I had come to the end of smothering those emotions. Emotions. They were alive and real. They refused to be silent. They popped out of nowhere and sat themselves down on the table in front of the jar—Buried emotions of the silent Child Within—*the child I had silenced was speaking.*

Echoing Silence—tears streaming down my cheeks, I sat in silence—

Listening. Thinking. Pondering. Meditating. Reflecting. Grieving.

I used the jar of pennies to organize, represent, and divide my entire life into time periods. It still amazes me that God knew exactly which coins I would need to visualize more than sixty years of my life. The fact that a gallon jar held the exact coins dated to span my entire life, and several from each year to represent specific memories that I needed to deal with, is something I look back on in wonder, awe, and worship. God cares about every detail. I had at least one penny for every year of my life except for five different years. The missing five years had dimes, nickels, or quarters.

The dates on every coin spelled out memories. Memories that were good and memories that were not good. I *sat* for months, day after day, taking specific allotted time frames each day, learning to embrace the painful memories and accept the emotions connected. I learned it was good and healthy for me to also embrace and accept the bright happy memories scattered across my life. Interestingly, the good memories were represented by coins that still had a shine. These were beautiful golden moments for me to treasure in my dark lonely journey. How good is God! He was with me, and He had not forgotten me.

I grieved the losses of childhood. This was a difficult time, but a very healing time. I began reconciling to God by fully embracing pain, experiencing pain, and allowing myself to feel the emotions connected to the memories instead of freezing off the parts of me I had deadened in order to survive. I had *chosen* to detach myself from the emotions at the time of abuse as my survival mode. This became my habit all through life. Living, but dead. To be fully alive means, I *choose* to feel, embrace, accept, acknowledge, and experience the emotion that belongs to every memory. Good or bad. I *chose* to allow myself to truly feel every emotion attached to every specific memory that I had buried.

I grieved the "*adultified*" child I became, the one who had to be so perfect and so good that no one would know her dirty secret. I sat with my inner child and we grieved our losses together. I learned to love that child and honor her tenacity, her strength, her courageous fight for existence, for life itself.

I honored her silence and the pain she felt when I buried her trying to destroy the person she was deep inside. I asked her forgiveness for closing off the parts of me that kept her locked up and isolated and in a deep dark prison. Together, we agreed to live, fully live life in full bloom, and to live life to the fullest potential with the identity of the unique creation of God. She was the soul He created for a purpose, He had thought of her, and He had a reason for her existence.

Pennies do not seem to have that much value or worth, but every 100 pennies equal a dollar bill. Dollars added together become tens, hundreds, thousands, millions, billions, etc. Our memories can be compared to a visual mental picture of a pile of pennies that keep growing from birth until we die. In that pile of pennies there will be good memories, and because this is life, there will be bad memories. What we do with those memories will greatly affect us—mind, body, and soul. This is how we as human beings were created. What we think about is who we become.

God created each person unique. We do not all respond the same to what happens in life, so our stored memory banks will have files that look completely different. My files were full of negative junk that was spilling out of the drawers. Messy. Broken.

Perhaps this is the reason Jesus says for us not to judge one another. I know nothing of every single detail of your life and why you react to triggers. Neither does any other person in the world know every detail of my life and why I react the way I do. Our Creator does know. I also know that God knows the plans He has for me. Those plans are not to hurt or destroy me. Or you.

You see, those pennies, beyond representing memories, were also the value my perpetrators placed on me, and then even those pennies were taken away. My value system was therefore reduced to less than a penny! And, in all of my life's journey that has been perhaps the biggest emotional roadblock to get around—valued for less than a penny—I am not worth even a penny! And is that God's value for me? Less than a penny? Such are the negative thought patterns.

God saw me during all the years that I stored up hundreds of millions of negative memories. He had a plan to give me hope and peace. Let's look at the results of negative thought patterns. How healthy do you think it was for me to constantly allow the thoughts of *"I am not good enough," "I am not loveable,"* and *"I can never do anything right"* to be the daily food for my thoughts?

These were just three of the negative thoughts that played over and over in my mind from childhood all through my life. Yes, bad things did happen to me. As a child, what I did not know was that I was not bad just because someone abused me. I was not abuse, but I thought I somehow deserved the abuse. These thoughts are real, and they will bring devastating results. God never created any of us to live life in fear and negativity. He created us to worship and love Him, and in doing so, we are free to co-create with God as the unique person He created.

How do I co-create with God? How do you co-create with God? Is this possible? Yes! God created our brains with the ability to bring our thoughts into captivity and be transformed by the renewing of our minds. How beautiful and rejuvenating it was to discover I could control my reactions to events and circumstances of life that were out of my control. I no longer had to see myself as the victim of childhood sexual abuse. I could develop my spirit by choices I was making in my mind. I was changing my brain, with my mind, by renewing my mind. (Romans 12:2)

The choice of renewing my mind was where the healing process would begin to redefine fears and reframe learned behaviors. The projected rage, shame, guilt, fear, and pain that had been absorbed into every fiber of the fabric of my being was now going to surface from the subconscious to the conscious. We will look later at the painful results of unresolved grief when my Grandma died.

I know this story is difficult to read at times. You have your journey.

Take Time. Ponder. Meditate. Process. Rest. Be Still. Be Quiet. Listen.

4

REDEFINING FEARS AND REFRAMING LEARNED BEHAVIORS

Confronting Projected Rage, Shame, Guilt, Fear and Pain

Trauma at 4 years old—

—I believed that I caused my Grandma's death.

I was an energetic child, and I had no time for lengthy periods of bathroom time. Chronic constipation plagued my body. I hated everyone telling me to *hurry up* because I was taking too long in the one and only bathroom. Fateful was the day at Grandma's house when I had to run inside to relieve myself. Bathrooms were not a place of privacy for the child in my home. So, when my Grandmother entered while I was sitting on the toilet and I heard the words, "Oh hurry, Honey, Grandma's awful sick", my stomach twisted into a knot. She sat down on the end of the old-fashioned tub, and then fainted falling backwards into the tub. I heard her head strike the tub with a sickening thud, and somehow the scalding hot water turned on at the same time. The hot water heater was sitting beside the tub, and it was always set on the highest setting. Instantly, scalding hot water was pouring between her legs.

I was a child. *Just four years old.* Forgetting my body needs, I jumped off the toilet and ran to tell my mother that Grandma fell in the tub. She ran to the bathroom to find Grandma sitting in a daze on the floor, soaking wet, hot water still pouring into the tub. Helping Grandma to her feet, my mother started to take off Grandma's wet dress only to see the skin coming off her mother's legs with the dress. Everything blurs for me. I hear loud voices, frantic cries of my mother's voice calling for help, and then words that seared my soul—"Why didn't you let Grandma on the toilet? You knew she was sick. You naughty girl! You hurt Grandma! Get away from Grandma!"

Fear. Rage. Shame. Guilt. Pain.

EMOTIONS NO CHILD CAN HOLD.

Grief and terror clutching my heart, soul, mind, body, I watch alone at the open window, tears streaming from my eyes as Grandma is carried to the car. I hear her groans. I hear her cries of agony. *My Fault*—I HURT GRANDMA.

I am alone. No one comes to comfort me. The house is quiet. I am alone with my brothers, little sister, and baby brother. Someone big is there, but I am *Alone. Afraid. Shamed. Guilty.*

I never saw Grandma again until we were in a funny place full of flowers. Grandma was in a bed with a lid, and there were flowers all around her. Everybody was crying and I could not understand why. I kept asking, "Why is Grandma sleeping in that bed?" I was told to be quiet. No one explained to me she was dead.

No. One. Held. Me. Instead, I heard over and over from my mother's lips the story that I was on the toilet and Grandma fell. And then I saw strange people looking at me. No one smiled. No one held me. No one told me it was *not* my fault.

I weep now as I write this story. I was so little. I was so vulnerable. I did not understand what was happening to me. I could *not* understand why I was so selfish and naughty. I loved my Grandma so much. I missed her. I could *not* understand why she was suddenly no longer at her house in the kitchen smiling and laughing while we made cookies together. I wanted her to hold me and read stories again. I wanted to see her dancing eyes and hear her say, "I love you, my sweet little Shari Cherry Pie." I ached to feel her strong arms holding me close, to feel her gentle rocking, to hear the goofy made-up songs she sang while looking deep into my eyes. *Safe.* I was safe in Grandma's arms—But Grandma was not there any longer.

My world was a very scary place. My grief was never processed. Loss was never acknowledged. I was made responsible for the grief. I was made responsible for the loss. I was *not* told that Grandma fell because she had a stroke, and with the third-degree burns, her body shut down fighting off many complications.

A child is not emotionally capable of absorbing this kind of trauma. Fear became my constant companion as I struggled to understand why my world had been turned upside down.

At this point I began to withdraw and imagine I was a perfect child who never did anything wrong and could never be punished. I thought if I could be a different little girl, and I could make Shari be invisible, then no one would be angry at me for *"making"* Grandma die. I did not know how to process the pain I felt from losing someone so dear to me. Added to that trauma, I felt rejected by those closest to me. And since I had no vocabulary to verbally describe how I felt, I did the only thing I could. I gave myself an ugly name—the worst I could think of—*Pearkin*. My family thought it was funny. I did not! They did not look for reasons or ask why I wanted that name instead of Shari. *Pearkin* was a shameful name—ugly, dirty, no good, not enough, liar, the girl nobody loved for who she was.

The stage was fully set for what was coming next—Grooming—Secrets—Special attention to a beautiful child starving for affection and acceptance.

Patterns of Learned Behaviors—Withdrawing—Perfection—Pretending—Walls—No Place to Cry—No Sense of Safety—No Place to Run—Always Hiding—Always Running Away—Always Seeking for Approval and Acceptance That I Am Good Enough to Be Loved.

Please, someone tell me I am NOT bad! NOT a naughty girl! NOT a liar!

The Child's Secret Soul Garden (continued)

Gardens are not complete without flowering trees. In the midst of the child's Soul Garden, the Master Creator Gardener had planted a tree that grew nowhere except in her soul. She was a soul created with thought and much care. This tree planted within her soul would never die. The tap root was connected to the source of Life, the Giver of Life from which flowed the Love of God. This tree of life was rightly named the Love Tree. Every potential of what would make up who she was, and the very essence of her inner being was the creation of God. He had created her totally unique and His plan was perfect.

The Spring of Life gurgling up near the base of the tree flowed into a never-ending fountain of joy that nourished and watered the many flowers growing throughout her Soul Garden. A cozy little nook held a wicker chair that she loved to curl up in and watch as the dancing droplets of joy touched every facet of who she was created to be. Her being pulsated with the joy of living.

Leaning back in the chair, she let her eyes feast on the gorgeous flowers above her head. The leaves couldn't hide the beautiful blending of colors hanging from the branches of goodness, faithfulness, gentleness, self-control, kindness, patience, peace, and joy. How could one tree hold so much beauty? There was nothing else like it in all the world except in her Soul Garden.

The Creator Gardener was the only one who could see the entire root system of the Love Tree. She was too small to know that the roots were connected to every part of her being, and they had been anchored there from the moment of her conception—unique to her. Every little tendril was part of her being—emotional, physical, sensory, mental, social, spiritual, and creative—she was mind, body, and soul. She was connected and aligned with the Creator Gardener. Her Soul Garden was connected to her Mind Garden which was connected to her Body Garden. Intertwined, interconnected, a perfect picture of entanglement—every aspect of her being in flow and at rest. Growing and thriving. A child full of potential and aspirations, dreams and desires. A creative, created child, ready to co-create with the Creator Gardener of her soul.

Her roots were anchored by thoughts, emotions, words, choices, and seeds dropped in her Soul Garden from the character traits in others. She learned to have faith, love, and acceptance by those closest to her. She was a child and absorbed everything into her Soul Garden. But the essence of who she was created to be would never change or be destroyed. Her thought patterns, her emotional stability, her choices would be influenced by others until she came to understand that choice had been her gift from birth.

It wasn't her choice to be carried into the shed. She had no way to stop the beasts from invading her sacred inner sanctuary. Her emotional being was powerless to halt the invasion. Helpless. Alone.

An internal earthquake, shaking the foundations of who she was created to be, cleaved the Love Tree above the ground into five separate trunks, yet the root system remained anchored deep in the essence of who she was. The Love Tree with the five trunks weren't noticeable to the naked eye. Invisible fractures of the soul, and no one could see the fracturing that had taken place in the inner fabric of her being, fractures that were deep in her mind. Fractured, broken, her flowers strewn throughout her Soul Garden, the child sat bewildered beside the clogged fountain of joy, weeping. A strange foreboding hung heavily in the air.

Toxic thoughts plagued her mind changing her emotional stability to toxic chaos. Depression clouded her mind, and her choices became toxic, affecting even her food choices, creating toxic habits that controlled her everyday life. Struggling to maintain her Soul Garden was draining off energy just to survive and keep a tight lid on toxic emotions that she had never experienced before.

Toxic Rage boiled deep at the heart of the split trunk sending signals throughout her body keeping her in fight and flight mode. Toxic Shame coursed through the tree sap poisoning the life blood necessary for the beautiful flowers that had been her crowning adornment. She watched in dismay as her Soul Garden disintegrated before her eyes as the Toxic Fear swept through her gardens enveloping and smothering every flower garden that she and the Creator Gardener had so carefully tended. Toxic Weeds of anger, control, mistrust, self-hate, worthlessness, resentment, aggression, discouragement, distress, dread, anxiousness, indecisiveness, hopelessness, fearfulness, suspicion, worry, shame, insecurity, inferiority, apprehension, withdrawal, hardening, and seething vengefulness sprang up out of nowhere. Growing into thick vines these

Toxic Weeds were climbing up into the five split trunks and choking out the lifegiving source coming up from the tap roots.

Toxic false guilt, pain, blame, and rage consumed every bit of energy from the sunshine she had stored and left her Soul Garden completely depleted of nutrients vital to health.

Toxic Fear had invaded her Soul Garden creating the atmosphere of death everywhere she looked.

The latch on the gate to the entrance of her Soul Garden had been broken beyond repair. The beasts could enter whenever they desired.

Grabbing up the broken mangled flowers of innocence, purity, and virtue, the child raced frantically to the inner sanctuary of her Soul Garden. Where could she hide her most treasured flowers? There was nothing left of her Soul garden but a trash heap! Hearing the beasts, she tried to dig in the soil, but the ground was suddenly hard and dry and her fingers too small to break the crust. She laid her flowers in a corner and piled debris around them, shielding the brokenness from more from destruction.

She could not let the beasts do more harm to who she was created to be! She could not let them destroy who she was! Where was safety? She ran to her favorite tree—the Love Tree. Shame washed over her as she tried to climb up the trunk and realized there were five trunks! Glancing down she saw a black hole at the center of the split leading straight down into the taproot of her core being. Safety was deep inside herself! The beasts could not reach her! There were no pennies to bring her shame.

But—*there were no flowers either.* Fear had blocked the light. Fear had silenced her sunshine song. Fear had invaded her safe place. Her Soul Garden had become the burial ground of hopes, dreams, aspirations.

As the cold winter snows covered the frozen ground of her Soul Garden blanketing the destruction within, the seeds planted by the Creator Gardener lay dormant, waiting.

Resurrection was coming because Life refused to die. The essence of who the child was, waited. The seeds of her soul, created by the Master Gardener, rested in the darkness of her Soul Garden, waiting.

No one to Care. Share. Bear. Take her heavy load of Shame, Fear, Guilt, Pain—And so, ...RAGE WAS BORN.

Rage that would form more patterns and learned behaviors, influencing her choices and inner struggles for life itself.

Why should she try? No one believes her anyway. Where is God? God is Love? He must not love her. What is love? What can she do to gain love and acceptance? Maybe work harder? Maybe take care of everybody? Maybe be the peacemaker? Maybe just do whatever she is told even if she does *not* like it?

Keep a bunch of *secrets* for other big people? Make them all look good? Because she is NOT A GOOD GIRL—she is *really, really* BAD. So BAD no one will EVER love her again if she tells. If she does tell anyone, she will be a LIAR because she is told that she "likes" doing BAD things. Things she does *not* understand. Things they tell her she likes to do—but SHE DOES NOT LIKE IT AT ALL!!!!!!

BAD—it was her fault Grandma died—or was it????

Pain. What is pain? How do you define an elusive shadow that grips the soul, mind, body, and spirit of the abused child? Where do the results and the effects of abuse lodge? How would you describe the painful shadow of shame that engulfs the soul, wrapping, entangling, entrenching itself and leaving its stain deep in the mind? It is a stain that shrouds her soul with a heavy dark blanket of false guilt. Her guilt? No.

Pain. The elusive shadow that squeezes the life from her soul. She tries to flee from it. The shadow follows her wherever she goes. The dark nameless something that plagues her nightmare dreams. That foreboding cloud that blocks the sunshine keeping her spirit in a suffocating death grip.

Pain. Shadows of the soul that suck her down to icy frozen depths. Relentless agony that slowly freezes her voice and silences her cry for help—the silent cry that shatters apart the already broken child. The cry that fragments who she was into so many parts that she does not know who she is.

Pain. She absorbs into every fiber of the fabric of her being everything she is told about *who she is*. She believes these lies with her head, but not with her heart, her soul, her mind, her spirit.

Pain. The monster that pursues and overshadows. What is this? It is generational abuse. Is she responsible for generations of adults who knowingly and unknowingly passed this pain to her? How is she, a child, going to stop the turning of gigantic wheels of time? How fast does she have to run to get away from something so massive it is impossible not to be crushed? She has no one to protect her from her abusers, so she chooses to protect herself by dissociation. She chooses this means of survival not knowing the price she will pay or the devastating results of her choice.

Pain. Shadows of time. Shadows. Now, she is an adult, a woman in her late thirties, frozen in time. The little child, who she *was*, stayed frozen deep within her inner being. She faces years of rage, shame, guilt, fear, and pain so integrated and entwined into her core being that she has no clue where to begin picking up the shards and fragments of broken messy.

Pain. Shadows. Silence. The adult fractured child now has a choice. Hard choice. Choosing to come together and to be the one unified unique person who God created her to be.

This choice starts the long process to bring unity at her core being. She begins the difficult task of redefining fears and reframing learned behaviors that no longer serve her.

Pain. Shadows that loomed on her own horizon. Her own doings! Her own children! She had tried desperately to shelter her own little ones from the pain she had suffered—not understanding or knowing that by running from her shadows she had done what generations before her had done!

Pain. Excruciating pain! *She was responsible for her decisions, her actions, her attitudes, her responses—Not her children! She was the one who had tried to love them in her own brokenness. Her efforts to shield them from pain—caused them pain! She had tried to stop the pain by running away from the pain!*

Pain. She had to stop running and embrace the pain she had refused to acknowledge all her life. Rage—that painful monster of abuse that had sought to destroy the person inside of her. The soul God had created. Rage projected on to her by others. Rage that penetrated her soul with unforgiveness. The dagger of unforgiveness cloaked in a sheath of pious good girl actions—disguising hatred toward a God who her "shamers" thought demanded perfection—before she, the child, could be forgiven or forgive others.

Rage. I was face to face with the greatest pain I had ever experienced. Rage was an emotion that surfaced throughout my life. I thought it was a spiritual issue and begged God to take away my besetting sin. I had no clue that this deep emotion was my blessing. My reason for tenacity. My reason why I clung to life with a death grip when I had no more strength to live.

Rage. Rage was the burning within my inner being that consumed my soul, demanding that justice be meted out to my perpetrators. Rage was my justifier. My excuse to blame. My reason to deny that I was responsible for my own healing from childhood sexual abuse. Rage that God would require me to do the difficult inner work of confronting the projected rage, shame, guilt, fear, and pain. Rage, that God expected me to redefine my fear and reframe my learned behaviors that I had absorbed from birth.

So, here I am, thirty years after the sexual abuse stopped, but thirty more years of continued verbal, emotional, spiritual abuse, and being confronted with the overwhelming task of fixing broken messy. How was I ever going to put myself back together again?—I felt like I was Humpty Dumpty in the nursery rhyme—he sat on the wall, he had a great fall, and all the king's horses and all the king's men could not put Humpty Dumpty together again! There was not enough glue in the world to put me together again.

Rage. How does God fix rage? He began by giving me a *choice*. Would I embrace this pain of rage and begin the healing process by renewing my mind, replacing negative thinking with His thoughts? Would I embrace the emotion of rage and embrace every painful memory attached to that emotion?

Soon we shall discover how the terrifying memory of a *Jar of Screws* surfaced from my subconscious, stared me right in the face, and brought me to the realization, that my *choice in that moment*—I was choosing *Life*, or I was choosing *Death*.

PART 2

REBIRTHING TO BE RECREATED WITH GOD

What is the core process of rebuilding our foundational principles to become the person God created each of us to be? It is a rebirthing process, and it cannot be hurried. It is messy, overwhelming, discouraging, terrifying, scary, and very hard work to go to the depths of a black abyss. We go there with the purpose to rebuild our core processes, reestablish belief systems, redefine our boundaries and every choice made at this point determines which direction the abused person will go.

These previous choices will bring us face to face with four definite life-changing questions: 1) Will I deal with this abuse and find my healing path to wholeness? 2) Will I run? As in choosing divorce, drugs, prostitution, alcohol, porn—anything that deadens the pain? 3) Will I act out my rage, shame, guilt, fear, and pain on others as in co-dependent behaviors to control others since I cannot control what is happening to me? 4) Will I destroy myself physically, mentally, spiritually, emotionally, or socially?

The nitty gritty core of rage is summed up in my belief systems in two questions. *Who is God to me? Where was God when bad things happen?* These questions bring us to choices that will determine the changes we make that directly affect and impact our destiny. Choosing is hard work. Choosing confronts ruin to rise, fully live, and discover there is beauty in ashes.

5

RECONNECTING TO THE REAL ME

Connecting Mind, Body, and Soul

The rebirthing process was slow and painful. It felt like jolting shocks of soul contractions as the memories began to resurface. I had buried and silenced the Child Within so deeply by closing off parts of me in order to survive. The fragmenting that took place was from choices made in my subconscious for survival. I still have no memories at ages where there should be vivid memories. I chose to separate myself. What was happening to my body was not happening to *me*.

The Child's Secret Soul Garden (continued)

The Love Tree continued to grow in the midst of the child's Soul Garden. Strange how the essence of who she was lay buried deep within, waiting. In the frozen depths of time, time for the Child Within stood still.

The five split trunks above the ground grew as any tree grows. There were years of drought, years of storms, years of hard winters, years of disease and pests that ate away the vitality of life. The trunks vied for the nutrients in the sap coming up from the taproot. Five trunks that looked like one trunk. Depending on what the circumstances of life presented to her Soul Garden, the trunks began to take on a weird twisting of values, thoughts, and behaviors. They obeyed the impulses and subtle cues of others and grew whatever form or mask they were told to wear. And the Child Within remained silent. Waiting.

Five trunks that had split deep in the emotional fabric of the Love Tree, producing instability where the child had been created with stability, strength, courage, and tenacity. Waiting. Living but slowly dying. Alive but frozen in the separation of mind and body. The Child Within. Waiting.

Her Soul Garden had fractured. The Child Within was waiting. Waiting and holding memories frozen in time. Her body holding memories. Her mind holding memories. Her soul holding memories.

Memories of a jar of screws. Memories of pennies. Memories of a beautiful Soul Garden. Waiting.

The Child Within waiting in her silent prison of Fear. Waiting for the adult woman she had been created to be—to come and set her free.

I write the next story *A Jar of Screws* in fragmented phrases on purpose to bring you, the reader, to a better understanding of what happens in the disconnecting of mind, body, and soul.

The journey to wholeness has many weird twists and turns. Memories will pop out of nowhere in the strangest moments that seem totally unrelated. For example, I was washing breakfast dishes one morning and enjoying watching the hummingbird at the feeder which was hanging outside the kitchen window. My hands were in the hot dishwater, I was watching the hummingbird—but, suddenly, I saw a jar of screws again. A jar of screws. On a shelf. On a wall with other jars. The water is hot, but my hands feel icy cold. I was enjoying a tiny bird—but now, I am seeing screws, and I am so terrified I am shaking and gasping for breath. I stand at the kitchen sink—frozen in fear as I stare at nothing—seeing screws!

I write this story in fragments because this is how the trauma surfaced for me. It did not show up all at once. God gave me what I could handle in the moment. This was the beginning process which would be working out over a period of weeks. Then into months and years. I was slowly choosing to allow myself to begin to feel the emotions that were attached to every memory of the trauma.

I will spare you all the details. Take a deep breath. Focus on the soul of the child as I tell you her story.

A Jar of Screws

A jar of screws . . . focus . . . on . . . one . . . screw. . . .

Grinder whirring near her head . . . big hand clamped over small mouth . . .

Searing ripping agony—*not her body*—floating—observing—*not her body*—suffocating—retching—white hot searing agony—*not her body*—*someone else*—*cannot touch me*—*safe outside body*—floating in black abyss—strong arms lifting body—do not look at body—*not her body*—choking—gasping for air—*and in the corner a jar of screws.*

—the beginning of many trips to that room of horrors—

Broken—Shattered—Pieces of Perfect—Who was she?—Where is she?—Where did the child go?—What was she like?—How can she find who she was?—Where did she go?—Was she a child a moment ago?—an eternity ago?—

Just one moment ago—an eternity ago—she—was—perfect—

But now—Shattered—Broken—Shards of whole—Slivers of perfect—

Which part of me goes where? Slivers of whole. Shards of perfectly created beauty. Who is this now? Where was God? Why was He not there? Why did He not protect her? Why did He not care?

Who is this? Does everyone see how dirty I am—Oh! *not me—not my body*—the dirty body is another girl—*not me*—where can I hide her—I cannot get her clean—I cannot wash away the smell—She is still dirty—

Who will believe *me*? Who will believe *her*? —

Pieces of what *was—the soul of a child*—

The shattered soul left with the lifelong task of searching for wholeness of mind, body, and soul. The soul whom God thought of at conception. Created by God Himself. His perfect thought and plan.

His smile of approval on His created being—and it was good.

Now this that remains—Good?

Broken—Good?

Shattered—Good?

Shards of what was—Good?

Is God *really* Good? Is God *really* Love? Is this all He thinks of His own created child? Is this His punishment for how bad a small child can be? Does God hate a child and let bad things happen because she is so naughty? A bad sinner?—and sinners cannot go to heaven.

Would she want to go to heaven if God is there? God is supposed to be her Father. Fathers are supposed to take care of their children—I must not be a good enough child—No one took care of me—I was not good enough for God—

I am bad—not good. How can I be good enough? If I hide the bad and just be good enough, maybe no one will notice I am dirty—not clean—smelly—cannot wash away smells—

Good—must be good—must do everything just right—Watching—waiting—running—working—cannot stop being good—just good—

Dark running shadows—shadows—*always* running with me—cannot stop working to be good—only good—cannot rest *ever*—must be good—must get clean—so dirty—running away from dirty—do not like names that stick—nasty names—run faster—work harder—smile more—laugh and act happy—work—cover up the dirty one—hide the naughty girl—work some more—

Do nice stuff for those big people—make them smile —get pennies—shiny pennies— "Shh—no one can know our 'secrets'—you get pennies, remember?" — "You're bad—naughty—no one likes you—only me"—dirty—run some more—smile—do not cry—you cannot cry—no one likes you—

"You are not worth even a penny—you cannot keep your pennies" — *"You better not tell!"*

Patterns of thoughts—Patterns of actions—Patterns of fractured existence.

Molding—forming the shattered soul into something she was not created to be. Smiles so bright on the outside. But a dark, a very dark shadowy abyss on the inside.

Alive with hopes and dreams, but deadened feelings within. Buried memories deep in every cell of her body—a mind fiercely blocking horror—agony of soul. Slowly freezing the inner self—to feel is to die.

Raging white hot anger rolling, tossing, tumbling beneath the frozen exterior.

Adult in a child's body. Innocence shattered, stolen. Secrets no child's mind, body, or soul can hold or guard. And then, she is required to keep a tight lid on the raging emotions that boil beneath the surface.

And so, that morning at the kitchen sink I made a tough choice. I chose to face the terror I had buried so many eons ago. I *chose* to allow the buried emotions to surface along with the memories. I was terrified. *But I had come to the place that I wanted life more than I wanted death. I COULD CHOOSE LIFE!!!*

I am choosing life, but how do I get back together again? Which part of me is ME? Where do I find who I was? All I could see was ruin and destruction. My whole inner being had been blown to bits. I had an internal warzone to clean up.

Who was I? Who am I? Am I still somewhere in all this ruin? I am thirty-seven years old at this time and trying to find the child whom I had hidden, buried within. She was elusive like a dancing whiff of smoke always just out of reach evading my grasp only to pop up and show her face in the weirdest of circumstances.

In despair and at the end of myself, I turned to God and said, "I *cannot* do this. I *cannot* put myself together. *I do not know how to be one person.*"

And God said, "*Choose.*"

And I said, "Choose?" "What do you mean—*Choose?*"

And God said, "*Choose.*"

And I knew to *choose*—hard choice—hard work—**And. God. Smiled.**

I was desperate for answers to the inner turmoil. I wanted relief from the constant pain that gnawed away at my soul. I was faced with a daunting task of reconnecting to the real me and I had no clue where to start. The God who created me knew the starting place. *Choice.*

My searching for answers led me to books. Self-help books. Books about trauma recovery. Books about co-dependency. Books about women's health. Books about abuse and stories of other survivors. Books about emotional abuse. Books about spiritual abuse. Books about marriage. Books for wives. Books about how to understand men. Books about childhood sexual abuse and trauma.

One hundred books and I am still searching for the answer—how do I reconnect to *ME*?

I read and reread every book I found. My library was growing. I have yellow highlights in every book. I found many helps. I began putting into practice every nugget that jumped off the pages and hugged me.

I was growing myself in many ways, but that little *elusive child* I was searching for evaded me like the plague—I thought. No, actually, she was so excited and happy to be showing me the way through the abysmal pit where I had locked her away. She was very tired of living life dead. *She* was the one who kept knocking on *my inner being* asking for freedom. She knew I was the one who had chosen to separate myself as my means of survival. She knew I had locked her away and silenced her. She knew where to find *the Good Enough Girl, the Good Girl, the Control Girl, the Invisible Girl, and the Silent Girl.* She knew why I had chosen each of those personalities. She knew I did not need them anymore.

And so, she whispered—*Choose ME! Choose ME!*

And so—*I chose ME!*

And—*I—Keep—Choosing—ME!*

We shall watch together how she takes *ME* to where the *Control Girl* and *Good Girl* are waiting to be Emancipated. First, I will let you read my poem entitled, *My Dance with God*. Then, I will tell you the story that is behind the poem.

6

RELINQUISHING TO BE RECONCILED TO GOD

Emancipating the *Control Girl Good Girl*

My Dance with God

I danced a dance alone with God one day,
Not a happy dance for all I had to say.
Where were you, God, on that horrific day?
Did you not see the crime committed as on that table I lay?
What audacity that I should hear you say—
I want *the Control Girl—Good Girl*—if I may?
God, you know dissociation was my survival name.
I was a child without control that day—you know I will
never be the same.
I am running from you, God—I do not want to play
your game.
I really hate you, God—you do not love me as you claim
Because all my life you've made me carry all this blame.
It's not fair I must surrender before you'll take away my shame.
Okay, God, you know I am not really
Good—Good is just a face;
I do not know who I am—my secret name is who
I will embrace.
My heart filled with golden light from the smile upon
God's face,

For in that moment I knew the wonder of His *Grace*.
God became my Father and His heart is my safe resting place,
And there I worship in the fullness of His *Truth* and *Grace*.
© Shari M. Rickenbach, 2017

And now, the rest of the story of *My Dance with God*. It is so amazing how God was working in my life, leading me step by step, taking me through the darkest night of my soul. I could not find God or sense Him anywhere. Reading my Bible was like sifting through chalk dust. Prayers fell silent on my lips. But my heart was reaching for the Light. What I did not understand was that God Himself was carrying me. He was holding me so close that I could not see His face or feel Him. He had drawn me into the stillness of His heart.

And in that stillness, His heart was whispering words of comfort to His broken child—ME.

But I could not hear His whispers of Love. My heart was boiling with a rage for which I had no remedy. Strange to say, my theology had no answer for what was boiling just under the surface of my frozen façade. Was this spiritual? In a way, yes, in a way, no.

We are spirit, mind, body, soul. Deep in my mind I desperately needed renewing. I had fractured, damaged emotions that simply had come to the end of being stifled—silenced. Emotions. They spoke loudly. Damaged emotions—they raged against the atrocities that had been inflicted upon my body. Silenced emotions—they spewed out like a mighty volcano, more than sixty years of pent-up white-hot rage.

I want to tell you more of the background story of *My Dance with God*. I struggled to find the answer to the deep rage that boiled at the center of my core being. I had no one I could talk to or express these horrible feelings to. I tried talking with a pastor and his wife at one point. There was much disconnect in our communications. He gave me the simple pat answer that my problems and difficulties were totally spiritual, I had left God somewhere, I had hidden unconfessed sin, and his *ultimate conclusion* of the matter was that *I was beyond hope!*

Before we judge too harshly the conclusions of this pastor, how many times do we all in one way or another do the same thing when we have no answer for the wounded hurting among us. There is a huge tribe of wounded souls who slip through the cracks in our churches, school systems, and medical diagnoses to give you a few examples. Damaged emotions are somewhere deep in the mind, and I searched desperately for the answers no one had to offer.

Theology and everything the church had to offer did not touch or heal the deep woundedness of my inner being. I had come to Jesus long ago even as a child and told Him all about my sin and asked His forgiveness. I loved Jesus! He never left me in my darkest hour even when life did not seem worth living. But God? I had such a huge disconnect with who God was to me! How could I love Jesus and hate God so much?

Ahh—My loving Heavenly Father! *He specializes in recreating wounded broken hearts!* He knew how fast I was running from my shadows. He knew when I would come to the end of myself. He knew how to draw my heart close to His heart. He used my art! He spoke to me of my own shadows as I worked on the shadows in an oil painting. He let me see that the shadows in the painting were what gave depth, intriguing beauty, and that arresting unique tonal quality that draws the viewer into the painting to discover more.

This is how much God loved me. This is how He showed me He is God. This is how He became my own Heavenly Father. This is how I know He is my God. *He drew me into Himself so that I could begin to see my shadows are what gives me the depth and quality of soul, mind, spirit, and body. I reconcile to God by embracing every shadow as part of who I am.* I can choose to be reconciled to God by the renewing of my mind through Christ Jesus.

I had been doing a lot of deep inner work. I was changing anything and everything in my daily habits and way of life that hindered growth spiritually, mentally, emotionally, physically, and socially. I was removing negative influences in every area of life. I wanted wholeness in everything—mind, body, soul.

My unplanned dance with God was coming up next, but I had no clue.

One morning after my husband left for work, I began putting the house in order for the day. I'd finished the dishes, wiped off the counters, and as I was finishing wiping off the table—the table suddenly was no longer my kitchen table—I was frozen—seeing myself—a very small child—tied to a shop table in a building far away. I stood there like a wax figure in a museum. Dishcloth in my hand, stuck in the motion, stuck in time.

Time. Time stood still. I saw her. I saw ME. I saw the child I was. I saw my buried emotions. I saw the child who could not hold those emotions. I saw Jesus standing there beside her, weeping, holding her emotions, holding the very essence of who she was. I saw Jesus placing her in the Father's hands to hold. And then, I saw God point to the helpless child on the table, tied. I heard the soft gentle whisper of God's heart. He said, "Shari, I want the Control Girl—Good Girl." God was Quiet. God Waited.

The volcano inside of me erupted. I ranted and raved at God for hours. I told God how much I hated Him for not stopping wicked men from acting out their evil deeds on a child. *ME.* A helpless little child. Where were you, God?

God listened. God waited. God looked. God loved. Quiet Stillness.

God filled—*Echoing Silence.* Quiet. Stillness.

My soul was quiet—*Echoing Silence* had spoken—My soul worshiped.

"Oh, Lord, You are my God. There is no other One who can still the raging sea. Okay, God, You may have *the Control Girl—Good Girl.* I relinquish her to You."

And—God—Smiled.

God's smile filled my inner being with golden Light.

The sunshine of His Love fills my empty void.

I have a Father who loves *ME.*

Just the way I am.

Just as I am.

Just who I am the way He made me.

God is my Father.

God is Love.

I have briefly touched the subject of Rage. This is difficult to put into words—what happens in the mind of the sexually abused child when her world collapses and there is no justice meted out.

The soul of a child is pure. Her virtue is her most priceless treasure. She does not understand that, nor could she put it into words. The grooming process is so insidious, and the innocence of the pure soul is preyed upon. She trusts with her whole being—spirit, mind, body, soul. So, when this child is alone with predators, given to them with permission to use her, she thinks God was the one who had betrayed, abandoned, and rejected her—a small helpless child left in circumstances far beyond her control.

My Dance with God, in a very inadequate way, describes my inner wrestling as I go to the bottom of the abyss and confront the core beliefs that I had formed about God. The fact that God would have the audacity to require me to relinquish *the Control Girl—Good Girl* impostor syndrome was totally outrageous and downright unjust of Him—I thought. How am I supposed to trust a God who allows this kind evil to be inflicted upon an innocent child? Why would I want to be reconciled to that kind of a God? What does "relinquishing to be reconciled to God" have to do with emancipating *the Control Girl—Good Girl?*

I wrestled with this inner turmoil. All my life. Outwardly, I loved God and served Him. Inwardly, I hated God. I loved Jesus and had accepted Him as my Savior—but I hated God. God was not my Father. I wanted to go to heaven and be with Jesus—but not God. I could tell others that Jesus loved them, died for them, and would live in their hearts if they asked Him to—but I had a difficult time talking about God's love. Oh, yes, I quoted John 3:16 many times. I had learned as a child that God loved the world, sent His Son into the world, and if we believed in Him, we would have eternal life. Amazing how I could separate not only myself, but God and Jesus. Jesus loves little children—I saw those pictures in the Bible story books and of course in Sunday School. But God? No, I could not wrap my head around the verses in the Bible that say God is Love.

Childhood sexual abuse is insidious in that it distorts who God is to the child. A child looks to those who are caretakers and sees them as God. They do not have the capabilities of separating those closest to them as being different from God. That is a scary responsibility. The child believes whatever has been told to them as truth. There is another added monster to this distortion, in that the child perceives and projects the evil of those who wronged them to be equal with God. This was my insidious sin that I confessed to God and asked for His forgiveness at the end of my dance with Him. *He was not mad at me. He loved me. He is God. He is Love. God is my Father. God loves ME!*

My dance with God was a huge step in this journey to wholeness. I felt so much better physically, emotionally, mentally, and spiritually for several days. I rejoiced to have gained a great victory in so many ways. I felt *healed. I needed those days of comfort, peace, and quietness of soul rest. It was easy to walk and talk with God early in the mornings in the dew kissed grass. The fellowship was sweet. My soul, mind, body, and spirit needed this refreshing time.*

I have mentioned throughout this story that the healing path to wholeness is a journey with many twists and turns that keep upsetting our equilibrium. I figured since I had done what God asked and relinquished *the Control Girl—Good Girl* that I was "good to go." After all, didn't I do something extremely difficult and straighten up a big mess in my beliefs about who God is? I mean, God really *is* my Father. I am feeling a security that I have never had. It is wonderful to feel loved and know God has got me—And God *did* love me, and He *does* love me. —And I *still* know He is my Father. And *because* God is my Father, He also knew how to redesign my thought patterns and reprogram my brain by replacing negative thinking patterns of abuse.

My big core issue of rage was centered on the fact my virtue had been stolen at a very young and impressionable age. My God issues were entangled in these beliefs that God just was not big enough to take care of me, and that He was not able to love me enough to protect me from evil men.

Now God would begin the process. Thankfully He did not show me the next thirty years of my life! I saw only the next step in front of me. That is all—one step.

You may be thinking, "Oh! I thought she was going to tell me five easy steps to heal myself!" *Emotional wholeness is never a one and done pill to swallow.* Every person is different. Uniquely created by God. Only God knows the path we individually take. Your path is not going to look anything like mine. *But you will discover wholeness tailor made for you.*

Loss of virtue was such an issue and influenced so many of my thought patterns and behaviors as you will see.

7

REDESIGNING THOUGHT PATTERNS—REPROGRAMMING THE BRAIN

Replacing Negative Thinking from Verbal Abuse

The Glorious Wedding Gown

I sat at the end of the pew next to the aisle and watched as my younger sister walked down the coveted bridal path, dropping her dainty fistfuls of bright pink rose petals. My eyes followed her journey to the front of the church where she turned with a beaming smile, triumphant in her accomplishment. All around me I heard whispers of admiration—She is so adorable—She is so cute—She is so sweet and dainty—She looks like an angel.

A dreadful gloom seized my young soul. I was not dainty. I was not cute. I was not angelic—I was the Liar—I was covered in shameful filth—I was not loveable—I was not good enough.

And then—the Bridal March! Here came the bride in all her filmy dazzling rustle of gauzy lace and satin! Awed by her beauty, my eyes drank in the glorious sight as the glowing creature floated down the aisle toward my spot. I could feel her joy pulsating, vibrating as she passed by me.

Realization settled over me and gripped my soul in a suffocating death blow—I *could never come to the altar* a *pure bride. I suddenly understood the significance of the white wedding gown. Purity. Virtue. I had been robbed of my most priceless gift I could present to my husband at the marriage altar! I could never give him that gift! My virtue had been stolen!*

Rage ignited in my soul as it dawned upon my young heart the truth of what had happened to me. Rage coursed through my body in white-hot flames moving swiftly—clawing, screaming, tumbling, jumbling, confusing, contorting, ripping, splintering, crumbling, pulverizing the fabric and foundations of my inner soul—billions and billions of fragments. Excruciating pain like a vice gripped my heart squeezing life from my hopes and dreams.

I sat frozen as thoughts raced through my mind like a train derailed, plunging off the tracks into black nothing—I could not wear a white wedding gown—I was not pure—I was a liar—I had a dirty secret—No one would love me—I was too filthy to wear a white wedding gown—I was just good enough for men to use me—pass me to someone else—I could never get clean again.

I watched as a man in front said things to the groom standing beside the bride. He said some words back. Then he said some words to the bride, and she said some words. I did not know what they meant. Then they kissed and turned around. The bride was smiling and the man beside her was smiling.

But—I—was not—smiling—

I was angry. *Very* angry. Suddenly I knew that man was going to take that beautiful bride away somewhere and *He—was—going—to—do—Bad—things—to—her—and—HURT—her! I MUST STOP HER!!!*

What could I do? —

"Hey, kids! Let's decorate their car while they are inside taking pictures. I will watch and tell you boys when I see someone coming!"

"Yeah, let's put stuff inside so they can't get in." "What shall we use?" "Hey, look at these tumbleweeds! They are huge!" "Perfect!" "Here is a big one! Help me stuff it in!"

In childish glee several little boys began working feverishly to get the deed done before any adults showed up to stop the prank. One little guy noticed a pile of mud clods, still wet, and grabbing as much as his hands could hold, he ran to the driver's side and dumped his load on the seat. The back seat was stuffed with prickly sticker tumble weeds. The front seat was on the way to being full when from the church steps I sounded the warning— "They are coming!"

I slipped inside the church and watched as angry adults surrounded the getaway car!

"Who did this!"

"You naughty boys!"

I was filled with a strange satisfaction as I watched from the safety of the quiet church six or seven little boys being disciplined. And best of all, during all the questioning they were pointing fingers at each other—forgetting that I was the one who had suggested the deed in the first place!

Ha! I got even with men! —little boys are like men! — *They* got in trouble—I did not—*They* had mud on them and stickers from tumbleweeds—I had a clean dress on. I was not dirty. *They* were. *They* had mud smears on their clothes and scratches on their arms from the tumbleweeds. I was clean—no dirt, no stickers, no scratches. *I paid men back! I got even! Big Win! —Maybe—*

This story is true. This is what I did at a wedding shortly after the time period when *The Jar of Screws* story took place. As I write these different stories, I find it quite revealing the dialog that surfaces and memories that pop out of nowhere. This truly is a journey to wholeness in every area of life. Because as these stories bring up circumstances and situations I had forgotten or buried, I now have the opportunity to deal with the residual negative thought patterns and behaviors that have influenced my choices for all my life. I have been on this recovery journey more than thirty years now at the time of this writing, and I have finally been able to accept the fact that I will be on this journey until I draw my last breath. I will always have life-changing choices to make every single day.

And so, I stopped to take a long deep look at my story of *The Glorious Wedding Gown* that I had just finished typing. I took time to ponder, muse, reflect, analyze, contemplate, study.

You do not know the buried thoughts and emotions that boiled within me that summer day. You do not know how these thoughts took root and entangled themselves in every part of the fabric of my emotional being. That entanglement is part of who I am today—an entanglement that is a massive labyrinth at my core.

I want you to understand and see in your mind what I am talking about, so I will paint a word picture to help you see the results of sexual abuse.

Scary Spiders and Their Webs

I am looking at sixty years of entanglement that has become so much of who I am, that it looks like a formidable fortress with a massive labyrinth of paths and secret corridors full of cobwebs and scary spiders to clean up and get rid of. And when I get one corridor cleaned out, I discover a few months or years later I missed seeing in the dark passageway, just one little spider ready to lay her eggs, and now the whole thing is full of spiders and cobwebs again!

I go searching in my library full of self-help books and find the book that has these perfect recipes and scientific formulas that spell out step by step how to get rid of all those spiders in one easy sweep! Great! Found the cure! I pull out the ingredients, sort them all out to make sure I've got this remedy right, mix it all up, and grab all my tools the book said were necessary.

I rush to the corridor where I saw the mess, thinking all the while, "I am going to destroy every single spider this time! I am so done with the pain all this causes me! And, I always get another bite from one of those nasty little creatures that leave me in pain for days and sometimes weeks! This is WAR on Spiders Day! When I get this taken care of, I will never have to worry about another spider bite!"

Full of vim and vigor, I am ready to tackle this job in one mighty sweep just as the book said! I race toward where I think the corridor is, and just as I get to the last turn, a gigantic tarantula grabs me with all eight of his sticky hairy legs, spins his web tight throughout my mind, faster than I can blink an eye!

"Ha! Think you'll get rid of those spidery negative thought patterns, do you, my Dear! Never! We *like* living in your mind! We are *quite comfortable* with the fine house you've built for us all these years."

"We have watched you getting ready for war. You want WAR, do you! Marshal the forces of negativity! Flood her mind with our negative power! Drown out her desire for thoughts that are lovely, of good report, uplifting, edifying, joyful, peaceful, and loving! Spray her down! Soak her!"

And all the little spidery negative thoughts rushed from their hiding places, swarming through my mind within nano seconds. Their cruel whispery voices were echoing from the deep recesses of my mind all the stored recorded files of verbal abuse, and my own resulting thought patterns. These negative spiders had been just watching and waiting for the right moment to appear so they could again pop open millions of files, and dump their loads, replaying every thought, word, action in nano seconds!

What fun the spiders were having as they scurried through my mind, whispering in great glee, watching as I again succumbed to the numbing effect of their poisonous fear darts!

"You're no good! Not good enough! Liar! Fat thing! You never can do anything right! Failure! You are so dumb! Who do you think you are! You dirty thing! You naughty girl! Nobody loves you! You are not a virgin! You do not have any friends! You are not worth even a penny! HAHA! Just look at you!

You thought today was WAR on Spider Day and just look at you! You are covered up with toxic negative thinking! You know you live in the Fear Zone which means you have chosen death! You would rather die. You are so full of fear. Ahh, my Dear, you know the Fear Zone is your home. This is where you have lived your life. No escape for you!"

But from another part of my mind I heard a quiet sweet voice gently say, "Calling from the Life Zone! Calling from the Life Zone! This is your new friend Dr. Caroline Leaf! You have been listening to my podcasts and reading my books. Now tell me in your own words what you have learned and have been putting into practice every day."

"Wow! How did I forget so quickly in the moment of overwhelm! Thank you, Dr Leaf! What I heard you say, when anything that is negative and toxic comes up from the past, the *first* thing to do is to be *grateful* that this ugly thing showed its face again! Because now, I know what to do! It is difficult to be *grateful* for this kind of pain! I am slowly learning that I have the opportunity to use *gratitude* as my sword against toxic fear."

"Dr. Leaf, I see the memory that came up has caused me so much pain that I have separated myself from the emotions attached to the memory. But, if I choose to embrace *both* the pain *and* the emotions of this memory *together* and *really feel* it, then I can get this toxic memory moved out of the fear zone where it causes me death. Yes, Dr. Leaf, and I remember you told me to pick up my sword of *gratitude* and be *grateful* that this toxic negative stuff in the Fear Zone has surfaced. I did not run away this time when I remembered the wedding gown. It is hard to *feel* the emotions that I felt as a child that day."

"Now, I am to *look* at it! *embrace* and *feel* the pain of the memory and allow myself to really feel all the emotions that are connected to this painful memory that came up! I am to be *thankful* and *grateful* that I know what to do with it! I am to be *grateful* that I have the opportunity to *look* at what has caused so much pain, *feel* the pain of the memory, *embrace* the pain *and* every emotion that is attached to that memory. Let me tell you something, Dr. Leaf! I just realized this has been the *key step* that I have missed for many years! I have always stumbled over this step, and at times I fell flat on my face. Embarrassing! *And,* Exciting! I can learn and change until I die! I am never too old to change!"

"Next, I am to give *praise* to my Creator that I can move this painful toxic memory with *every* painful emotion attached to it over into the Love Zone-Life Zone where God is. In the Love Light of His thoughts, I can now bring these tormenting thoughts into captivity that keep me a prisoner of toxic fear. I am the one who has the strength and power through Christ Jesus to break down and set myself free from toxic fear, and I do it with *gratitude and praise and worship*! Now, I know what to do with anything toxic and negative in my life."

"At last, I am ready to *worship* my Creator God who loves me and delights in co-creating with me. God created me to worship Him! I *worship* Him knowing that my inner-core-being is transformed moment by moment as I bring every thought into captivity."

"*This is how I experience lasting transformation.* God created me with this ability to bring every thought into captivity every 10 seconds and renew my mind in Christ Jesus."

"Thank you, Dr. Leaf, for showing me how to move forward on my journey to wholeness! These lessons are so simple to apply every moment of every day!"

I am always amazed when I look back over the last thirty years of this healing journey. There are so many bright nuggets of gold that God dropped right in my hands. Just when I needed them. Dr Caroline Leaf is a jewel straight from heaven. Recently, I discovered this lovely lady. I found her books, podcasts, blog, and YouTube videos to be exactly the tools I needed to do the difficult work in finding my own answers to many questions. Some questions are answered by asking a question for every answer we give as we are doing the deep inner work of soul healing. Nobody on earth truly has the answers for the questions we ask ourselves as we search through the labyrinth of damaged emotions. Only God does.

I love the study of neuroscience, and I discovered the most fascinating teacher in Dr. Caroline Leaf. She explains things that are so complex and makes them simple to understand. True, when I listened to her videos, she gave so much information that I could not digest it all, nor does she expect anyone to be able to grasp it all at once. That is why she has written so many books. I knew what she had to say was the huge missing piece of my puzzle in putting this inner brokenness together. For that reason, I invested in myself by investing in her programs and books. I knew this information was my answer to freeing myself from the effects of the trauma I experienced.

God had already been telling me to choose. Healing of my emotions really is my choice. I am responsible for my own actions. Dr. Leaf makes it simple. We think. We feel. We choose. That's it! This is the nitty gritty of tough healing. We take the toxic fears and negativity that surface and reconceptualize the thoughts and feelings of emotional pain. We feel it deeply by embracing this pain, choosing to be grateful that we know what to do with this toxicity. We praise our Creator for the healing journey and then worship Him in the Love Zone where He takes all that toxicity and transforms it by the renewing of our minds. In this we have Life abundant!

We are choosing to think negative thoughts, or we are choosing to think uplifting nurturing thoughts. Negativity opens the door in our minds to allow toxic thinking. And toxic thinking destroys brains cells and causes so many physical difficulties. Trauma does too.

When I was sixteen years old, I had horrible headaches for months. I missed a whole quarter of the school year. The headaches were so excruciating that the doctors did brain scans to see if I had a brain tumor. I will never forget hearing the doctor ask my mother if I had been drinking a lot or using drugs. The answer was no, as I have never tasted alcohol of any kind ever in my life or used drugs. Yet, brain scans showed holes in my brain as if I had been an alcoholic for years!

Then, later in life, I find out that trauma does the same thing! Our bodies do keep score. Interestingly, no doctor asked me if I had any trauma issues that I needed to talk about. Only one professional ever asked me if something bad had ever happened to me. This was when I was about ten years old. Only one! My parents took me to a chiropractor because my nose would twitch in a weird way. He was a truly kind man, and his question was so gentle that I almost spilled the whole sordid mess that day. But fear kept me silent.

Perhaps, this is why the journey to wholeness of mind, body, and soul looks to the abused person like this meandering senseless trail of tangled wilderness where she goes in circles, going off on tangents, seemingly on a journey to nowhere.

The black abyss is deep in the mind. The child's mind cannot hold the horrors of what is being inflicted upon her body. She is told this is love, and yet love hurts. The emotional ambivalence of love/hate, pain/pleasure, fear/trust, acceptance/rejection, shame/honor, rage/peace, guilt/innocence, all these conflicting emotions happening at the same time wreak havoc deep in the mind, body, and soul of the child. She has no way to process the trauma that is taking place, so she stores these memories, buries them deep in every cell of her body.

Throughout her life, the body first begins to lift its voice to be heard by using illness, aches, and pain to get her attention. Remember, I told you my body was plagued by constipation already at four years old. I was the first to get measles, mumps, chicken pox—anything contagious. I was usually the first in my family to succumb to whatever illness was going around.

My body spoke louder at sixteen with the headaches. At that time, I really had no desire to live, to fight my way alone through the devastation of my mind, body, and soul. I still kept my dirty secret buried deep within. I did not know my illnesses were actually speaking to the trauma. I ignored what my body was saying, because after all, if I could not voice the trauma and despair I held within, why should my body have voice? I did not realize I was choosing to die, and that I was giving my body permission to attack itself rather than face the effects of what the trauma had done to my mind, body, and soul.

What and how we think and the thoughts we allow in our minds directly affect the body as a whole. We cannot separate mind, body, and soul. Healing begins in the mind by redesigning thought patterns, by reprogramming the brain to think differently, to change mindsets, and to change the negative thinking patterns that are so grooved in the brain as residual debris left from physical, mental, emotional, verbal, sensory, spiritual, or sexual abuse. We do this by bringing our thoughts into captivity and renewing our minds through Christ Jesus.

I know that I have taken more time in this chapter to lay the groundwork for the rest of this book, but I think you will understand better as we move on and start *confronting the ruin to rise.*

8

REFINING PROCESS TO REORGANIZE MINDSETS, HABITS, BEHAVIORS

Confronting the Ruin to Rise

Imagine with me that we are standing halfway up on a mountainside, and we are looking down into a luscious green valley garbed in all its Spring beauty. As far as we can see all through the valley is a sea of cherry trees in full bloom. We are drinking in the beauty, captivated by a something that arrests the eye, but we are not sure what it is that is drawing us into the picture spread out before us.

And then, we notice something at the edge of the little village. Covered in vines and surrounded with cherry blossoms, our eyes focus on the ruins of an old brick church that did not survive an earthquake many generations ago. What is it that is so fascinating about the scene? The ruin. It is the ruin that arrests the eye and gives character to the whole. Without the ruin, it is just a pretty picture. It does not stir the emotions of the viewer, drawing them in to contemplate, ponder, wonder, grieve for what was, feeling sorrow that such a beautiful building now lies in ruin.

The picture is a figure of the true. We see a valley full of grace and lovely lightness, but the depth of character lies in the ruin that is graced in fragrant beauty.

Life is more than what meets the eye. The beauty that we see in the Spring comes after the cold and snows of Winter. The winter seasons of life bury the hopes and dreams of every one of us. God has not forgotten us. Underneath the cold layers of snow, life is stirring, waiting for the Spring to melt away what seems like death. This time of darkness and waiting is the season we do not understand. We are alone and isolated, smothered in layers of rejections, trials, illnesses, mis-understandings, betrayals, losses, sorrows, griefs, and painful circumstances.

Then comes the springtime warmth. We think, "Ah, warmth!" But the trouble that caused us grief has not floated off as the morning mist. Life is stirring within, and we feel a turning of our captivity away from the cold frozen prison of Winter. But there is still something stark in the landscape of our life like the ruin of an old crumbling building in the middle of beauty.

There is a fact, a truth, a memory, a possibility of what could have been that looms up and demands that we face it. That knot of painful circumstances that lodged deep in us is still there. That fear, that fearful thing, that waits like a starving leopard just waiting to spring upon an unsuspecting fawn. These things still are. It would be a lie to pretend and act as though they were not.

That page of life that we so desperately want to rip out and destroy can never be removed. It is still there in all its ugliness. It will remain engraved in the fabric of our being exactly how it is. Ruin. There will never be any changing of fact. Truth. Reality. It just is. Ruin is part of the landscape of life. However, *ruin is not the end of the story! Every one of us was created with choice. Choice!*

I am the one who has the freedom to *choose what I will do with what remains! The ruin. What do I do with the residual of ruin? Is ruin who I am? Is ruin my identity?*
OUT OF THE RUIN I RISE!

Choice is the beautiful gift I give myself over and over again! Confronting ruin to rise is my pivotal point in the refining process. I told you the story of *The Glorious Wedding Gown* for a purpose.

The rage that festered in my mind, body, and soul from the time I was eight years old into my mid-forties was what kept my internal foundations shaking. This rage, over the ruin that I had to take care of, sucked out all the energy required to do the difficult internal emotional work. I had no answers for how to fix what I was left with. Ruin. I looked to other people to do the fixing for me, and in the process, I was sucking all their energy out of them. I was angry, and they were angry. I did not know why I was angry, and they did not know why they were angry. Have you ever experienced this?

I was confronted with the rage that boiled because virtue had been stolen from me. My most priceless possession was taken by force from me when I was a small helpless child. No one fought for me. No one protected me. No one cared. Confronting ruin came with four very clear choices:

1. Will I deal with this abuse and find my healing path to wholeness?

2. Will I run? As in choosing divorce, drugs, alcohol, prostitution, porn? —anything that deadens this pain.

3. Will I act out my rage, shame, guilt, fear, and pain on others as in co-dependent behaviors to control others since I cannot control what is happening to me?

4. Will I destroy myself physically, mentally, spiritually, emotionally, or socially?

This was the tough test in the pivotal moment!

I *chose* to go with the first one on the list. I *chose* to deal with the abuse, *confronting the ruin to rise*. I wanted to be free. But freedom always has a price tag. That cost is humility. As

I stated in chapter 2, *humility is action in full motion when we, as abuse victims, receive and accept the fact that I am not responsible for what happened to me, but I am responsible for what I do with who I am as a person.*

Will I take responsibility for my own actions, behaviors, thoughts and feelings, my choices for how I have lived life? I cannot project my rage on others. I own this rage. Am I justified in this rage? Yes and no.

Yes, in that what happened to me was wrong and a crime was committed against a child. And not one single person confessed to the crime.

No, in that I cannot be justified by projecting my rage on others and have them act out that rage for me, and they in turn project on someone else. This is the nitty gritty of generational abuse. No one will take responsibility for their actions, and yet they expect and demand the next generation to fix the rage, shame, guilt, fear, and pain they carry. It will not be fixed. We do not fix anything by projecting our pain onto someone else. I take responsibility for what I am responsible for. I am responsible for ME! I stop generational abuse by taking responsibility for my actions.

I *think* about what has happened. I *feel* every emotion that is attached to every trauma. I *choose* to move all this destruction and ruin and toxicity into the Love Zone–Life Zone where God is. *Relinquishing this rage is my right and my choice. This is the choice that keeps moving and keeps propelling me within the healing stream of God's Forgiveness and Grace.*

I want to pause a moment and consider *forgiveness* and *grace*. These are two shiny gold nuggets I found, and I will never let go of. They are in my treasure chest of tools that I use frequently. These nuggets of real value have added value every time I pick them up and use them. They shine even brighter when I wash them with my tears! As a side note, I confess to you that I find I need to use forgiveness and grace every moment of every day!

Forgiveness is a choice. It has nothing to do with how I feel. *Forgiveness is a choice.* Period. *A Choice.* It is a *choice* I make every time something negative pops out of nowhere to dance through my mind and plague me with all sorts of scenarios. I find when I *choose* to give a dose of grace along with unconditional love, the pain I feel in the situation or circumstance loses its sting.

Forgiveness never means we condone the wrong done to us. Forgiveness never means we have to forget about what was done or excuse the person who did the wrong. Forgiveness *also* never means we hold someone else accountable. Forgiveness *does* mean I release myself from being a prisoner of someone else in my own mind. *Forgiveness is the gift I give someone else only to discover I released myself from my own captivity. Forgiveness sets me free.*

The refining process seems to have no rhyme or reason to the searching soul who has been abused. The memories are so random and come up at such unexpected moments. It is difficult to separate the past from the present. The triggers that pop the raw ugly into the happy, quiet, even worshipful times are strange and weird moments seemingly totally unrelated. These triggers keep the internal earthquake shaking the foundations from the core being. It is this internal shifting that moves and cracks her outer shell, her walls, her masks, or whatever form of protection the Child Within has built for her survival. *Only her own choices can remove the prison walls she has constructed.*

Choosing to reorganize her mindsets, and to change learned behaviors and habits is exhausting difficult work. But, as she confronts the devastating results of ruin and chooses each possibility of change, by acting, she steps from dark despair into life itself.

I began this chapter by painting for you the word picture of the broken ruined old church that did not survive an earthquake. How does that story connect to confronting the generational abuse by addressing rage and forgiveness?

This may be painful for some of my readers to swallow, let alone digest. Many of us grew up in a church, and we were taught beliefs about God. For some of us who understand the repercussions of generational abuse, I am positive you have already grasped what I am talking about and where I am going now. For those of you who grew up in loving stable homes, I invite you to come and sit a spell in a space where many of us have lived all our lives. We do need you. We need to know what safety and stability was like for you. We will learn to create our own space of safety and stability as we heal ourselves and move forward in life. We need to learn new behaviors and patterns. We want to model what you have lived out so that we will not pass our brokenness to the next generation.

And so, let us all take a walk down into the village. We need to explore that broken-down old church together because we are all hurting. There really is not much left of it. The generations before us have not even tried to fix it up. It is pretty much just a pile of rubble. What do you see? What causes you the most pain? What questions have you always wanted answered?

How were you treated when you did ask from a hurting broken heart? Was there anyone you could go to for help with your problems? Were you afraid you would be ridiculed, shamed, or worse, shunned? In the pain of your abuse, did you ever try to talk to the pastor or some church leader about the rage you did not know what to do with? Did they listen, really listen to your broken heart?

Did anyone enter into your suffering and weep with you? Or just sit with you in your grief over your loss of childhood? Did anyone tell you it was not your fault? Did anyone let you know they cared about you, even if they did not have the answers to your questions?

What are we going to do with this ruin and devastation? We can blame our parents, grandparents, greats, and great-great-greats—or, we can do something different. Together we can confront this ruin to rise. Right where we are, in our circles of influence, we can make a difference and stop generational abuse. We can make all kinds of excuses for ourselves for not changing our behaviors and habits and mindsets that keep us locked in a downward spiral—or, *we can choose to think the lovely thoughts that enhance, enrich, and nourish our starving souls.* We can deny that we have any problems and believe everybody around us is the cause of our grief and pain—or, we can say, "*Whoa, I am done living like this! I am out of this victim B.E.D.! In fact, it is high time to burn it! I do not need to be a victim of anybody, not even of myself.*"

The Child's Secret Soul Garden and Inner Sanctuary (continued)

The Inner Sanctuary of the Child's Secret Soul Garden lay in broken decaying ruin. Every year the rubble of her Soul Garden grew as she added memory after memory to the burial grounds of the Sanctuary. How was it that the place of exquisite beauty that the Child had been created with could become the burial grounds for unresolved trauma all through her life into adulthood? She had buried and silenced the Child Within many years before. The silenced child had no voice as the results of reoccurring trauma were dumped upon her—smothering and burying her deeper under layers of icy frozen Fear.

Underneath the frozen layers, the Child Within waited. Waited for the Creator Gardener to melt the icy coldness of her burial chamber. She was alive, but she was living dead. Waiting. Hope stirred as she watched her now *adult self*— walking into the broken-down sanctuary of the Church in the Valley. Today, perhaps today, someone would turn and smile at her and maybe, just maybe the ice jam would break in her Inner Sanctuary and allow the fountain of joy to bubble forth again. Maybe she could feel again the warm loving smile of the Creator Gardener as she sat trying to worship in the Church in the Valley. She remembered the whole valley used to be full of Grace and lovely Light. But, as she gazed around inside the sanctuary, all she could see was the ruin of her own Inner Sanctuary.

Where was the Creator Gardener? Would He come again to the Inner Sanctuary where He had made her Secret Soul Garden so beautiful? How she longed for the sunshine of His Love and Grace. He had met with her so many times in her Secret Soul Garden and had showed her how to make each flower garden breathtakingly beautiful. She had so loved the worship times. Her whole life had been in tune with the frequency of worship because that's how she had been created. To worship the Master Creator Gardener was the essence and flow of her life.

She bowed her head, tears flowing down her cheeks. She thought about her broken and ruined Inner Sanctuary. She realized it was impossible for her to repair the emotional damage of trauma. Grief-stricken, the *adult woman*, pondered how she would ever be able to melt the layers of frozen rejections, trials, misunderstandings, betrayals, losses, sorrows, griefs, and painful circumstances. Did she really *have* to keep the Child Within buried as her means of survival? *She* wasn't a child any longer, but the *child* who she *had been*, remained frozen and buried. How was *she* going to reach through to where her Child Within was waiting?

She longed for someone to come and sit beside her on the pew. Her isolated lonely life had become overwhelming. Was there *any* person in whom she could confide? And, if there were someone, would they truly understand the emotional devastation and ruin that she was looking at in her Inner Sanctuary?

Fear raised his mocking head and then jumped on her shoulders. In a sarcastic whispery voice, he dumped his load of negative words straight into both of her ears. In desperation, she cried out, "Master Creator Gardener! Help me!"

A Presence drew near. It was the Master Creator Gardener! She fell at His feet and worshiped. He was the One she longed for! He alone could fix her broken ruined Soul Garden! *The broken ruined Church in the Valley was her own heart garden!* The Creator Gardener had returned to dwell within her Inner Sanctuary! Her Soul Garden was her Inner Sanctuary! She bowed in worship as the Love of the Master Creator Gardener filled her Soul Garden with Light!

What do you say? What do you think? What if as a mighty army we do the tough boot-camp internal emotional work? What if together we open our hearts to the Master Creator Artist and give Him the brush of our lives and ask Him to transform the ruin of our life canvases? We have all made a mess and ruined what He created in us, and He is waiting to show us who He created us to be. He made every one of us totally unique, and He alone knows how to fill the void in our souls.

I need to explain a lot more about the victim B.E.D. of Blame, Excuses, and Denial, so we shall move on and explore what is necessary to realign our belief systems. This is the bootcamp of confronting the ruin to rise! Together we shall rise! I am in the trenches with you!

PART 3

RECLAIMING BY REHARMONIZING TO SING GOD'S FREQUENCY

Part 3 is the stage set for action. The sexually abused child has no good anchor point to look back to in her life and say that a certain point was normal. She has no clue what normal was supposed to look like. She only knows what was normal for her. Her belief systems are twisted, she does not know her identity, she does not know what forgiveness is, and neither can she fathom that there is such a thing as unconditional love. Discovering that pain is her gift and tool to finding her worth, value, and voice is beyond her comprehension. Her heart was made to sing with God, to sing His frequency. Let's examine the breathtakingly beautiful stages of metamorphosis as we watch the fragile butterfly emerge from her cocoon.

9

RENEWING MY MIND

Realigning Belief Systems by Choosing to Burn
My Victim B.E.D.

The journey to wholeness is like peeling off many layers of an onion, and onions usually cause tears. This process is painful as we return to the place in our memories where our souls died. We experience the same feelings, and the emotional pain is still excruciating; we smell the same smells locked in time; we see vivid colors, faces, the exact location the trauma occurred; we hear the voices of our perpetrators—we relive the trauma in detail as if it was happening right now.

We would rather this part of the journey did not have to be visited, but it is a necessary part of healing. We are returning to face the eternity where time stood still. The Child Within never moved beyond this point in time. We go there to sit with her *in* her pain. We go there to *feel* her pain with her. We go to *grieve* her losses. We go to *comfort* the Child Within who knew no comfort in the long ago forever moment, the moment that has been forever recorded in her memory. She may not recall every detail, but her body has remembered every single detail that her mind blocked out.

This moment in time has anchored her. She is still a victim. How does she move from victim to victor? Is this possible? YES! *It is choice.* This anchor point where she changes from victim to victor is perhaps the most excruciatingly painful part of healing. She makes the choice to get out of B.E.D.—her B.E.D. of *blame, excuses, and denial.* This will be her deciding anchor point that releases her into freedom to renew her mind and realign belief systems. By choosing to get out of her victim B.E.D., she is like the fragile butterfly that knows when to leave its chrysalis.

The struggle for freedom is necessary to develop the butterfly's wings so she can fly. And, so it is when she leaves her prison of silence others who are watching are tempted to give her answers, directions, and advice, but only *she* knows how to break out of her bondage and set the *Child Within* free. This struggle is necessary, no matter how painful it is to watch. It may take months or even years in the recovery process before she is strong enough to fly. Interfering with the progress may stunt her development for the rest of her life just like the butterfly who will never be able to soar. Her greatest need is the nourishment of unconditional love and forgiveness.

Now that I have set the stage for this chapter, I will weave in two more stories to give you a glimpse into what my healing journey looked like. Please understand that my stories can never be your stories. My prayer through this whole book is that the things I talk about will open the door for you to have a better understanding of your own traumas, giving you the courage and hope necessary to move fully into your own healing path.

I began this chapter by telling you that the journey to wholeness is like peeling off many layers of an onion. And if you have ever peeled an onion, you know that most of the time you will begin to cry. Emotional healing comes slowly. We would love for the process to be easy and certainly not messy or painful. After all, haven't we endured enough pain throughout life?

My layers were being peeled back slowly and they popped off sometimes in chunks and pieces. Sometimes it felt like a knife gouged deeply into my core being and a surgical procedure was being performed without anesthesia. I felt numb, bleeding, raw. I wondered if this journey was worth it—the longer I was traveling this way, the worse the pain got. This cancerous something had eaten into the very marrow and core of my being. I did not know how to get rid of it.

One thing I did know—I had a gift built into my character because I had fought with everything in me just to survive from one day to the next. Your *gift*, you ask? Yes, my *gift*— *Tenacity*. I was determined I was going to find answers and do whatever it took to find wholeness of mind, body, and soul.

The experiences of life cast strange shadows into our minds, especially if there is abuse in any form. It is that fact, that truth, that memory, that possibility of what could have been that is looming up, demanding we face it. So, we each have a choice. We can start peeling off the onion layers by asking ourselves questions and for every answer to the question, ask another question until we get down to the core root issue of what we need to confront.

Will I continue to embrace my victim stance—keep making my victim B.E.D. of Blame. Excuses. Denial.—as my forever home? What will it look like for me to burn that B.E.D.? Do I really need it? Is it a convenient crutch that is so comfortable to lean on? Do I really want to continue using blame as my cop-out to excuse my habits and behaviors that keep me swathed in layers of *band-aids* and in denial of the gaping wounds in my soul?

I wonder what it would look like to be free of this comfortable B.E.D.? Comfortable? How comfortable is a B.E.D. that has a mattress full of rocks—sticks and stones that broke my bones—those sharp words of verbal abuse that cut and keep hacking away at my subconscious causing my soul hemorrhage—is this how I want to finish life?

I had a personal *choice* to confront the ruin that was causing my soul to continue hemorrhaging. The process of getting to the bottom of the pain took time and daily bringing my thoughts into captivity by refusing to continue the *blame, excuses, and denial* game. Every moment of every day was my *now moment* for change. *Disciplining my mind to change the negative thinking patterns that kept me locked in a downward spiral became my march in an upward forward direction.*

The Memory Lane Trip

Traveling through memory lane was not exactly the vacation trip I wanted to take. However, God had something He wanted me to confront. He first woke me up one morning around 2:00 a.m. I was terrified to see in front of me a picture of an old wooden building. Remember the double exposure images that film could take on the old cameras? I saw half of the building. My bedroom was dark, but I saw full color! I choked out a whispered prayer, "God, you have been with me so far on this journey. I want healing for this emotional pain. If there is something I need to see, I know you will be with me." Instantly, I saw the inside of the building. It was the place I never wanted to see again. The place I had buried along with my *inner child.*

I cried and talked to God for two hours. Finally, I reached over and awoke my husband. I knew I had to tell him what I was seeing and what had transpired. Nineteen years of marriage and he had never heard what I was about to tell him! I was terrified! I knew he loved me, but I was terrified to open my heart to this kind of pain. We cried together as I described in detail what I was remembering and everything that I had suffered on that horrific day—the day my soul died.

I told him that I needed to return to that place of torment in person and confront terror face to face. So, we made plans to make an exceptionally long trip that summer. I had not been to this location for more than thirty years and really had no idea if the building was still standing. We agreed that it was necessary to revisit memory lane together. This journey was about me, but it was very much about us as a married couple and as parents. Yes, it was time to confront the monster that was trying to destroy us as a family. We would join forces and do this unified.

We drove onto the property, and *the building* came into view as we came up the drive. I felt like a sledgehammer had struck my lungs! I could not breathe! I sat staring, not moving, frozen in time! My husband went to the door of the house to let the owners know we were there. He chatted a bit with the couple giving me a few minutes to get my equilibrium. I felt numb. Weird. I could not stop crying. And so, my husband explained to the couple, who were complete strangers, that this visit was something very emotional for me. The lady hugged me, told me to make myself at home, and take all the time I needed.

We walked toward the dreaded building that was *exactly* how I had described it in the early morning hours to my husband. My heart was pounding out of my chest.

I stepped slowly through the open doorway and stopped—Right in front of me was *the same table—same grinder—same jars of screws on the wall—same smell of oil, grime, dirt.*

Up in the rafters was the old bedframe which I had also described to my husband.

Truth. Truth. Fact. Fact.

Fear that had waited like a starving leopard ready to spring upon an unsuspecting fawn—*that fear turned and ran out the door!*

I walked boldly over to the place of torment. I had a quiet talk with God. I placed my hands upon the spot where I had been so long ago.

I said to the *Child Within,* "Sweetie, I am here now. I am taking care of you now. You are not alone anymore. We are together. Jesus was right here with us that day. He did not leave us. God was crying. It hurt Him to see what wicked men would do to a child. He loved you that day. He cared about you that day. We were not alone. Sweetie, I love you. You were such a brave little girl. *You do not have to dissociate any more. We can be one person now. I came back to our place of fear. It is time to give this to God and leave these memories in the Love Zone-Life Zone where God is. Together, you and I, we choose Life. Together, we choose to live life to the fullest. Together, we choose to align in God's creative design for our life.*"

And so, in *choosing* to burn her victim B.E.D, she *chose* to be a victor. She *chose* to be one person and allow the Inner Child to live life to her fullest potential because she had found her purpose, her why, her reason for existence on this earth.

The Inner Child Image

I close my eyes, and this image floats beside me. I turn and focus on a small shadowy form walking toward me in the misty foggy morning. The form draws near, and I see a small child holding out her arms, pleading for me to pick her up. I reach for her, and she leaps into my arms. Snuggling her head on my shoulder, her small body convulses in sobs as she wraps her little arms around my neck in a death grip.

Her story spills from quivering lips, and the words that pour from the gaping wound in her heart tear my heart wide open. We are one in our grief. Our tears flow together and mingle with the gall of anguish as we sob out the *Echoing Silence* from the depths of our aching abyss.

What is this? The *silenced inner child* has come back into her soul! The child, now calmed and comforted, lifts her head to the morning light breaking through the misty dawn. Her tiny hands softly pat my cheeks, wiping away my tears. Looking deeply into my eyes she whispers, "Look! Look to the Light! Look at the Sun of Righteousness! Look at Him in whom there is no shadow of turning!"

We turn to the Light and see the Author of Light, who was the Creator of Light, who is the Sun of Righteousness, and who is the Son of God Himself! Together, we, the woman and the child, reach out to grasp the hands of the One who has been walking the whole long journey with us all through life. Hand in hand, we three, are made one. The child, the woman, the Creator of life.

I watch, as one, they step forward into fullness and abundance, vibrancy of wholeness in a new creative life aligned in the Creative Divine Designer Himself.

Together, as one, they, the woman and the child, step into the flow of the purpose, *the why*, the reason for their existence on earth.

Clothed in honor and dignity, with new life pulsating from every fiber of her being, she, the woman and the child, as one, step forward through the open door set before them.

She moves now with the graceful ease of the conquering victor, overcoming fear and obstacles thrown in her path to wholeness. She runs swiftly, straight to the black yawning abyss where millions of silenced children, enslaved as trafficked victims of the sex trade, are groping in the darkness for an open door, seeking for a way out of their fear and despair.

At the brink of the abyss, she throws herself down on the very edge, forgetting herself. As she reaches deep into the pit and grasps the first hand of the child reaching for her, a joyful song bursts from her lips and the *Echoing Silence hushes!*

From the depths, the dungeon walls begin to reverberate with the frequency of hope! The sweet refrain that is echoing back from the depths are the millions of child sex slaves singing as they each clasp the hand next to them and reach deeper into the pit for the hand closest. They have formed a mighty army! The song swells to a mighty psalm of praise as they sing their deliverance anthem of victory that was written from selections taken from Psalm 24 and Isaiah 30:15.

Deliverance Psalm of Victory

In confidence and quietness shall be our strength!
Amen! Amen! And Amen!
The Lord of Hosts is strong and mighty in battle,
The Lord mighty in battle!
Who is this King of Glory?
The Lord strong and mighty in battle!
Amen! Amen! And Amen!
Lift up your heads, oh gates,
Lift them up, you everlasting doors!
And the King of Glory shall come in!
Amen! Amen! And Amen!
Who is this King of Glory?
The Lord of Hosts!
He is the King of Glory!
Amen! Amen! And Amen!

And so, we come to the end of another chapter, but it is the beginning of a new chapter in her life as she moves forward into unexplored territory. She has burned her victim B.E.D. of *blame, excuses, and denial,* and now with life pulsating in every fiber of her being, she looks around in delight at the vastness spread out before her. This is a panoramic view she has never seen before. Oh, she had caught tiny glimpses of what could be, but her B.E.D. had distorted her vision of brand-new possibilities in rich experiences that would expand her soul, bringing healing of mind, body, and soul.

Not knowing where to begin her adventure, she paused, drinking in the beauty. Noticing a gate in a wall, she was seized with great compelling desire to work in a garden and grow beautiful flowers. She thought about a garden that had been destroyed and buried somewhere in her memory so long ago. She loved flowers, especially the flowers of her soul that had been so ruthlessly destroyed.

Suddenly she ran toward the gate in the wall. She *had* to see what was on the other side!

10

RECLAIMING TO REHARMONIZE

Embracing My True Identity by Accepting My Secret Name from God

The Secret Garden!

Her fingers trembling with excitement, she fumbled with the latch on the gate in the wall. What was on the other side! This gate was familiar! She recognized something vaguely, but there were so many vines entangled over the gate she wondered if this was real! Wondering why she had forgotten this entrance into what she vaguely recalled was a garden, she leaned into the resistance. At last, yielding to her desire to see beyond, and slowly creaking open on rusty hinges, the gate of her memory swung open.

Her breath caught in dismay at the sight of what once had been the most exquisite secret garden God had created uniquely in her. In great sorrow, tears streaming down her cheeks, she entered quietly, reverently, grief-stricken, moving slowly through what had been her very own garden—the exquisite garden of a child's soul, *her* soul.

She, the adult woman, crumpled in a heap on the ground, staring in numb anguish at the ruin spread out before her. Sensing a movement beside her she turned and saw the Child Within tiptoeing near. She held out her arms and drew the child onto her lap. Holding the little form close to her heart, their tears mingled as one. In the *Echoing Silence* of the soul, they sat in stillness.

As the soul of the child grew quiet, I grew quiet. My soul was hushed. Comforted and safe, the child lifted her face to mine. Looking deep into my tear-filled eyes and in a choking voice the child said, "I tried to fix it up, but you held back your tears for so many years my flowers could not grow. The weeds always took over, and you made the ground so hard with your rage that I could not yank out the roots. They just kept growing and getting worse. I do not know how to make it beautiful again. I am so tired of doing it all alone."

"I know, Sweetie. I am really tired too. Will you forgive me for making you do this inner work all alone? I am so sorry for treating you like this. I gave you an impossible job to do. I made you to be a victim all my life, but now I am changing how I used to do messy broken. I buried all my emotions trying to smother the life out of you.

"Sweetie, I need your forgiveness for treating you so horribly. You did not deserve this kind of treatment. This was not how God created us. He did not plan for all this mess. I need God's forgiveness most of all. It is hard to forgive myself, but I must start here. Forgiveness will bring the dews and rains of repentance, and God will wash away the dry hardness of my soul with His everlasting love. This is where we can start together again and make our secret garden full of beautiful flowers. Together, Sweetie, you and I, we are going to reclaim this garden and invite the Master Creator Gardener of our soul to dwell here with us. He is going to help us root out the weeds of rage, shame, guilt, fear, and pain of generational abuse. I am choosing to take responsibility for my own actions and realign to who God created me to be."

At this confession, the Child Within leaped for joy! Dancing in glee she twirled in the ecstasy of reclaimed childhood. Excitedly she grabbed for my hand. "Come! Come and see the inner treasures of us that I hid! I rescued every flower, every facet of who we are and who God created us to be. I would not let you destroy who we are! Come! See where I buried us! I think you will have to do the digging though. It is pretty hard for me to uncover and fix what you did as an adult. I could not figure out why you would cover up all the soul flowers I tried to plant and grow. You would never let the sunshine of Love warm the seeds I planted when you kept them clouded with all your negative thought patterns."

Hopping and skipping beside me, we, the child and I, explored the secret garden of our soul. This place that needed reclaiming was now ours to dig through and toss out what no longer allowed us to live life in full bloom to our fullest potential.

We began to be grateful every time fear popped its ugly head out of the ground. We looked at each other, the child and I, and thought about why fear would be presenting itself again in this situation. The child was much more adept at pointing out where I had buried toxicity. She reminded me that she had tried many times to tell me I needed to deal with what I kept shoving aside and trying to bury. It was so difficult to take ownership and be accountable for my actions. I really did have to take responsibility for what I had done. Slowly, I realized that she, the child, was pointing me to my weapon for reclaiming our garden! *This weapon—this tool—this golden key was hidden in my mind!*

The golden key to recovery and healing depended on my own focused choices. Focused discipline would stop the patterns of negative thinking that were destroying brain cells and keeping my whole body infused with toxicity. Toxic fear was literally causing death in me. I had lived my whole life in fear. It was going to take lots of discipline to bring my thoughts into captivity and renew my mind in Christ every moment of every day! I was going to constantly use this tool—this golden key—my O.A.R. of ownership, accountability, and responsibility!

We walked slowly through what was once the garden in the soul of the child I buried. I looked with dismay at the entangled vines and roots of rage, shame, guilt, fear, and pain. Tears streamed down my cheeks in torrents of grief and sorrow. Strangely, there was a shift in the atmosphere of my heart garden. The air that had been heavy with despair, depression, anxiety, negativity, and thoughts controlled by fear began to lift off as a morning fog clears in the sunshine. The sunshine revealed a hidden clump of something that had been tossed over on a trash heap. Wondering what could be struggling to grow under the pile of filth, we stepped carefully around brokenness. Then, I saw it—my core issue. I saw what I had fought for, searched for, grieved for—wanting to reclaim, to bring back, to find again, but it was gone forever. My flowers—*gift of virtue and purity*.

The child and I walked over immediately to where we saw my trampled and besmirched flowers, *gift of virtue and purity*, lying shriveled and broken on the ground. It was not my fault virtue had been robbed and tossed aside as worthless. We stood there looking at what had been our most prized possession—*our gift that we were saving for the one man who would love us unconditionally*—the man I would someday marry. We both reached to tenderly, gently pick up what had been. With a lump in my throat and tears coursing from my eyes and heart, I hugged the pain of what was—what I could never give to the man I loved. I allowed myself to feel, really feel, the emotions of betrayal, abandonment, shame, guilt, fear, rage, grief, and sorrow.

Holding what was—what had been—we knelt on the ground.

Quietness. Stillness. Thinking. Feeling. Choosing. Choosing Life. Worshiping. Waiting. Being still and knowing He is God.

I heard a rustle and felt Someone beside me. I turned and saw the Creator Gardener of my soul. He drew near and sat with me in my grief. Gently, I placed my deepest grief and pain in His nail-scarred hands. My soul poured out the words I could not speak with my lips. He sat quietly, listening, nodding, understanding, feeling my pain—knowing my pain.

Quiet stillness slowly filled the aching void. I waited for Him to speak, but only quiet stillness filled the garden of my soul. Comforted, I rested in the quiet. Waiting. Worshiping my Creator.

And then, I heard the quiet words, *"Would you like to have my virtue? My virtue is everything you will ever need. In Me, you will have no lack. I will never leave you or forsake you. You are mine, Child. No one can ever take you out of my hand. I am your God. I am merciful, gracious, long-suffering, and abundant in goodness and truth. I keep mercy for thousands, forgiving iniquity and transgressions and sin. I am the Eternal Self-Existent One. I am the Eternal Creator of all things. I am full of tenderness and compassion.*

I am full of goodness and love. I am very patient. I am abundant. I am the Good God who is the Bountiful Being—I am exuberant in my beneficence. I am Truth. I am the Truthful God, the One who can neither deceive nor be deceived, who is the fountain of truth. I am the Keeping God, keeping mercy for thousands of generations, showing compassion and mercy while the world endures. I am the Redeemer, the Pardoner, the Forgiver, the Being whose prerogative alone it is to forgive sin and save the soul. I am the Righteous Judge, who distributes justice with an impartial hand, with whom no innocent person can ever be condemned. I am the Vengeful God who visits iniquity, who punishes transgressors, and from whose justice no sinner can escape because I am the God of retributive and vindictive justice. This is who I AM. I AM your God. I Am Love. I Am Life. I fill every aching void of your soul with all this. This is my Virtue and everything I AM is yours. Choose Life and you choose Me. I am your Lord. I am your God."

I bowed at His feet and worshiped. Quiet.

"My Lord and my God, I worship You. You are my Everything. You are all I need. *Yes, Lord, I accept Your Virtue. I choose Life—Life abundant. I choose You.*"

We walked together through my garden. It looked different when the Creator of Life walked with me. There was sunshine everywhere. The sorrow, grief and pain were transformed to joy. I began to understand that the pain had been working for my good. I remembered the names I used to have and wondered if those could be transformed too. So, I asked the Gardener what I should do to change all the ugly stuff that had kept my heart garden locked up.

He smiled and nodded in agreement. Yes, it was time for a name change. It was mine to accept, but it came with a choice. *A choice I would make every single day for the rest of my life.* The Creator God explained that the name change He had for me would be like the garment of praise I would choose to put on each morning. *I would choose to clothe my soul and guard my heart and mind by bringing my thoughts into captivity every moment of every day.* I would be living out my Secret Name. I would be walking in my Secret Name.

I did have another choice to make first. If I wanted this new Secret Name that was just for me, I needed to write down all the other names that I had embraced as mine throughout life. These were names that did not belong to me. Names that I wore as a mask. I had so many masks that there were days I had worn several at the same time trying to cover up all my pain.

I couldn't remember *not* having a mask close by. I was quite uncomfortable as I thought about each name that I wrote down. These names were so familiar. I automatically wore whatever someone else had told me to pick up and put on, covering up their pain, shame, guilt, blame, rage, fear—whatever came up, I was to act out for another person and make it mine. I wore their mask as mine.

My list was getting long and filling up the page. Finally, I put the pen down, and looked into the Gardener Creator's eyes. I saw that He was pleased with my honesty. He smiled His approval and then pointed to a cross in another garden. The Garden of Gethsemane. Now, I had a choice. Would I take all those false names that did not belong to me, take them to the cross where Christ Jesus had paid the ultimate sacrifice, and let Him nail those names to His cross? I had to leave them all there with Him. I could not take any of those names off the cross and wear them as mine if I wanted a new Secret Name—the Secret Name God had given me before I was born. It was mine to claim. But, first, I would choose to leave behind all the names God had not created me with. Names that were not my identity.

I did *not* know who I was. I did *not* have my own identity. Was it possible I could have my own identity in Christ Jesus and have a new Secret Name? Yes! I would take this difficult step. It was scary to walk away from my comfort zone of pain. I did *not* know any other way to exist. I had no idea what to expect.

Who was I without pain, shame, guilt, fear, and blame? I ran all the way back to the garden of my soul. My heart felt light and free! I had never felt this way before! The Gardener's joyful laugh rang out through the garden, and my soul echoed the same joy. Unspeakable Joy was bubbling up within me in a never-ending Spring of Life Eternal. I was ready for my name change!

I stood in the middle of my heart garden looking at all the broken messy. I still had no idea how to fix it. The task before me was overwhelming. Somehow, this name change must be part of the answer I was looking for.

Expectantly, quietly, I waited.

The Creator whispered, "Your name is Grace."

Grace is who you are in Christ. Let me tell you who you are, Grace. You are Gracious, Joy, Merciful, Tenderness,

Compassion, Loving-Kindness, Elegance, Acceptance, Precious, Pleasant, Well-Favored, Pleasure, Delight, Sweetness, Charm, Loveliness, Goodness, Love, Patient, Truthful, Exuberant, Bountiful, Forgiver, Besought, Fair, Considerate, Giving.

You are Shari, *Song of God.* You are mine. You are loved. You are worthy.

I walked into soul freedom by embracing my true identity in Christ Jesus. Accepting the name God has given me is to experience reharmonizing joy unspeakable. *I reclaimed who I am in Christ and found my soul was brought into harmony with the frequency of God Himself.* I worship Him who is my Heavenly Father. He is my God and I now live and move and have my being in Him who gave Himself for me on the cross.

Reclaiming to reharmonize with God by embracing my true identity in Christ brought me to the place of accepting my Secret Name of Grace.

I had no idea how much Grace I was going to put on every day as I began to reach through pain to redemptive hope. We are soon going to find two golden keys. Two keys I would need to keep polished with much use every day. *The golden keys of relentless forgiveness and unconditional love.*

My tears of repentance would be softening the soil of my emotional being. I would be embracing the pain and reconnecting to the emotions that I felt when the flower of purity was destroyed. I was embarking on a journey to wholeness through the deepest and darkest valley I had ever seen.

11

REACHING THROUGH PAIN
TO REDEMPTIVE HOPE

Finding Freedom Keys of Relentless Forgiveness
and Unconditional Love

The path to wholeness will always lead us to the place of our deepest pain in the deepest abysmal pit. We go to confront the pain, the soul agony, the place our soul died. We finally arrive there, the bottom. We see the ruin, the broken messy, and we sit with our grief. What *was*—is what *is*. There is no changing that can bring back what *was*. That person is gone. Lost forever in her very long-ago eternity. If virtue is stolen, there is no restoring her most priceless gift she was guarding for her husband. Her gift is gone. This is her core issue.

This is where her rage boils up out of nowhere. This is her place of fear. This is her shame. This is her guilt. This is her pain. This is her prison. But was it hers? How does she reach through that pain to redemptive hope? What is the secret to finding her freedom keys of relentless forgiveness and unconditional love? How does reaching through pain to get a hold of relentless forgiveness and unconditional love—*by embracing the truth of* brokenness—open her heart to a flowing river of hope, mercy, and compassion?

Perhaps the best way to open the door into a healing path is to talk about how undealt with painful traumas affect all marriages. Marriage has its own unique set of difficulties as two individuals endeavor to blend their lives as a couple. We all bring our old baggage into the marriage. Abuse adds another bitter taste to what should really be delightful and a wonderful adventure for two people who have pledged themselves to love and to cherish the other until death. Our vows included for better or for worse, in sickness and in health. We meant every word that we said on that beautiful June day.

However, our story line got messed up. Healing comes randomly. We live life together and those nasty buried memories that we think love will cover and heal, suddenly pop themselves into our conversations and many times they twist, turning into full-blown arguments. We draw away from each other in our corners wondering why we ever thought this person we sleep with every night could be so different in the blink of an eye. What is wrong? Then we go further and even question why we married them in the first place.

We wonder why it is so difficult to freely love this other person we have joined ourselves to. Marriage is a beautiful bond between husband and wife. He complements and adds dimensions to her inner growth that makes her wonder how she ever lived life without him. She was created to give the balance a man needs in the emotional realm that enhances his masculinity and strengthens his abilities to carry out the difficult decisions a man must live with. We were made to enrich, nourish, and empower each other and live life to our fullest potential. She as total woman and he as total man.

However, abuse disrupts this beautiful harmony called marriage. Trust at some point was destroyed with abuse. We view life with different filters. We somehow want another person to fix the aching void we feel deep inside. We may not say those words exactly, but our actions and thought patterns take us down that road. No other person can fix the damage done during abuse. *It is our choice as victims to either dive deep into the pain and begin healing ourselves, or we go through life demanding that others stop the hemorrhaging of our soul.*

Much damage occurs in a marriage if the person who was sexually abused demands the spouse to stop their soul from hemorrhaging. They cannot.

And so, I will tell you the word picture I wrote to my husband 19 years into our marriage. We celebrated our 45th anniversary this year as I am writing our story. It is possible to stay married and heal the wounds. God knew we needed each other to make it through this journey. God knew my husband was the one who would bring out the worst in me so that I would deal with it, and yet he would love me as if I was doing my best. That is the real nitty gritty definition of unconditional love. He loved me when he had to *choose* to love me. Not because I was being so gracious, he just could not help but love me! No, I learned from my husband what real unconditional love is. He also chose to forgive me. No matter how rotten our day had been, he has every single night for 45 years, rolled over, wrapped me in his arms, kissed me, and said four beautiful words—"I love you, Shari."

Can you believe that I would keep the secret of childhood sexual abuse from my husband for 19 whole years? He could not figure me out. I could not figure me out either! I have told you the story in bits and pieces up until this chapter.

Imagine what it would have been like if you had lived with me not knowing what you do now. What would your reactions have been if you would have had to confront the horrors with me if you had been my husband?

Now, look at those you love and who you rub elbows with every day. And the love of your life whom you kiss goodnight and hug every morning as you leave for work. Maybe they seem to be holding you at arm's length and you do not know why. Have you ever wondered if they could be possibly hiding a horrible secret from childhood because they do not know if you will continue to love unconditionally?

Neither of us understood what the healing journey was going to look like. Maybe, as a man thinks, he thought this abuse could fit nicely into that compartment like his, hoping I had one in my brain too. And we would just pop this junk into the file, shut the door tight, out of sight out of mind, and we'd be happily married ever after as in all fairy tales. Not So! Nope! This wife of his was a completely different creature!

If he thought our "discussions" would be ended in two sentences, he was left scratching head four to six hours later wondering how we'd gone in circles, and he kept bumping up against some kind of hardness in me that hurt! In his masculine way, he usually had some ready solutions and answers for me that if I would just *listen* to for once, I would not have so many difficulties—life really ought to be easier than this. And no, I was not about to take his answers for me because I knew I was hiding pain deep inside of me. I did not think he could look at that kind of ruin and still love me. Besides, he thought he had married a virgin. How was I going to tell the full story and not have him walk out of my life—I had deceived him for 19 years, remember? And so, I wrote him a love letter in the form of a word picture that I entitled, *The Marriage Garden.* I will share the story with you.

The Marriage Garden

The child and I, together, have been working daily in our secret garden. It really is becoming a beautiful spot. We have imagined all sorts of ways to enhance the loveliness within. This is our work in progress. We have tried so hard to cover up our pain and allow others to see only the beautiful parts, and we have been hoping to prove to anyone peeking over the wall that we are doing a great job being a wife and mother.

However, there is the one spot in the garden that we have kept hidden behind very thick walls for a real good reason. We need to let you in on our secret so that you can understand better what you haven't figured out.

Many years ago, the Child Within and I, together, built a very strong fortress that was impenetrable for any man who sought entrance. No man was allowed access to this part of our heart garden. The walls were high and overgrown with vines of distrust, anger, rage, anxiety, and fear. The inner core garden gate had a rusty lock that was corroded with broken abusive relationships. The corrosion had eaten away the boundaries so many times the gate was hanging by hinges that were falling off. All that kept the gate intact was the thick wall of vines that blocked the gate from view. We did not want you to find the gate. And yet, what you do not understand, we *wanted* you to find the gate. Every time you have come anywhere near this gate—the entrance to our inner core, the true authentic buried person we are—fear rose up and walled you off in a hard resistance that you could not define. Fear refused to let us trust you.

We need to ask your forgiveness for withholding our love from you. That has hurt you dreadfully.

I do not want any other man to see the mess that I have been hiding from you. You are the only man who has ever cared and proved to us—this Child Within and this woman you married—that you meant three words—I love *you*! We so desperately needed to know these words were ours to accept without obligations or requirements attached. You have proved over and over to us that you mean it when you say, "I love *you*, Shari!"

You have been God's gift to us. You did not know when you married us that we were more than one person, but you loved us until we could blend back into the one person God

107

created your wife to be. She *chose* to be one person. She did the difficult inner work, and you loved her through all the upheaval until she could get there. You are a one-of-a-kind husband, and I am so very blessed to call you mine!

Now, let me tell you about the mystery that has been hidden behind the facade, the masks, the personalities I wore as mine. This wall you have bumped up against for 19 years of marriage is thick, and I did not know how to tear it down.

I will show you where the gate is. I am *choosing* to chop down the entangling vine of fear first. I will begin with a mighty whack and confess that I am terrified. I am terrified that once you know what is beyond the gate, you might leave me, abandon me, or abuse me to punish me for deceiving you for so long. The second whack is to tell you I was not the virgin you thought I was—I was robbed of virtue. The third whack is to tell you the source of my rage—I hate God because He did not protect me, and I do not trust God or you.

There, the gate swings open! Do you want to see what lies hidden?

His tear-filled eyes looking deep into my soul, his gentle clasp on my hand was the answer I needed. I swung open my inner core being and allowed my husband entrance. His breath caught at the ruin. He saw. He understood my fear, my shame, my blame, my guilt, my rage, my pain.

We cried together. We grieved our loss together. We understood he had been robbed, too.

We, husband and wife, walked softly, reverently, quietly to the place where we, the child and I, had buried and hidden from sight our most fragile flower of purity.

He, her husband, saw how we, the child and I, had tried to rescue our most prized flower, watering it with our tears, guarding it fiercely, but nurturing and cultivating pain with bitterness against God. It had been worth more than all the rubies in the world. *Our loss was great. Robbed, virtue stolen and tossed aside as if it were worthless. This was her core issue.*

Fear had stopped her emotional growth and kept her locked in silence. Locked in an Echoing Silence that had walled out the person she loved the most—her husband.

Kneeling quietly in her inner heart garden, her husband tenderly, gently lifted the fragile broken flower of purity to his lips. Kissing the broken messy and holding it close in his heart he spoke with deep emotion. "You are the most beautiful woman in all the world. If I had known about this broken inner garden before we were married, my sweet, lovely little wife, I would have married you anyway. You, my love, were not to blame. You, my sweetheart, did not deserve this shame. You, my most precious treasure, are a virtuous woman. Your price is far above rubies. I love you and *only* you. I ask your forgiveness for not understanding what you tried to tell me so many times."

They, the husband and wife, renewed their wedding vows and pledged again to love each other until death parted them. This lifelong commitment to each other was reinforced by their words of affirmation, each taking ownership for their own actions and responses, each being accountable for doing their own 100% to make their marriage work, and each taking responsibility to change themselves as individuals. By changing themselves, they would change their marriage and rebuild the foundational structure of their home. They were in this together. They were committed to make their marriage work by never taking the victim stance and blaming the other person.

Their Marriage Garden was being transformed day by day as they made tough decisions and chose to love unconditionally and forgive relentlessly. Their hearts were bonded together in a love that held them steady when the fierce winds of adversity threatened to tear them apart. No way were they going to allow their love to die! This was the kind of love they pledged their faith and trust in. It was the Love of God being lived out on a daily basis in their home, in their hearts.

These decisions came with a price. *They both had to lay aside their expectations and preconceived notions that the other person was responsible for their happiness.* No, the voids in the inner core being of both husband and wife would be filled with God who was their Heavenly Father. They learned quickly they had a lot of bad habits and ways of communicating that needed to be brought into alignment with who God created them to be.

Changing the inner core was going to take concentrated work and effort. They would make plenty of mistakes, but with the golden keys of relentless forgiveness and unconditional love, their love was renewed and strengthened. They were like newlyweds!

They remembered again all the beautiful character traits they had seen in the other person when they first met! They found the secret to keeping love alive was by thinking, feeling, and choosing to live in the Love Zone-Life Zone where God is. God is Love. His love taught them how to love each other and rebuild those broken communication lines between them.

The inner core garden of her, the wife, was still in shambles. Trust would grow between husband and wife, but it would be a slow process. Trust was a deep root that had developed with a weird twist. All her relationships were tainted with an unnamed something that held her back from developing lasting friendships.

Outwardly she was vivacious, likable, lovable, bubbly, sunshiny, gracious, and a sensitive listener. Inwardly, the inner chaos was draining the soul life out. She had years of hard work ahead. But her gift of Tenacity for life abundant was going to help her through difficult situations. Tenacity would keep her focused on taking the one next best step ahead on her healing journey.

Those taints from the past would be transformed and lose their toxicity as the couple, husband and wife, in a brand-new relationship, began to rebuild their fractured marriage.

Choosing to change required moving through the deep pain they had caused each other. *They quit blaming each other for relationship issues. They quit making excuses for their behaviors, they quit denying they had difficulties between them as a couple.* They burned their victim B.E.D. of *blame, excuses, and denial* and each picked up their O.A.R. of *ownership, accountability, and responsibility.*

Together, they, the husband and wife, as one, began to row the canoe of life in beautiful harmony. There would be rough waters. There would be rapids and whirlpools that tried to drag them back into crazy eights. They would run into underwater snags that caught them and dumped their canoe. They did not quit. They learned to laugh at their bedraggled tear-soaked mess and try again to do this tough thing called marriage. They were going to make it together. *They were choosing to love anyway and do this together for life!*

They, the husband and wife, were learning progress is a lifelong process. *They were choosing every single day to reach through pain to redemptive hope by using their freedom keys of relentless forgiveness and unconditional love. They were created for each other and together they would co-create with God.*

And so, we conclude this chapter of her life. Honestly, she has in all reality just opened the door to her authentic healing journey. She does not know at this point that she is on a journey. She is still hoping that all these changes in her inner core will magically remove the pain. She is still avoiding the surgeon's knife. There is a putrid cancerous growth from generational abuse permeating every fiber of her being, and only the Creator Gardener could do the surgery that was required.

Her healing path to wholeness is found in choosing. First, she will be *thinking* about the toxicity that comes up in situations that serve as triggers from the past. Second, she will be *feeling* the pain of the trauma and every emotion connected to the pain and fully experiencing the connection of pain and emotion together. Third, she will be *choosing* to be grateful for this pain. *By choosing gratitude, she discovers hidden treasure.* This treasure will be mined out as she retunes her soul to sing God's frequency with the song of gratitude. We will sing this song with her when she discovers pain is her gift and tool to worth, value, and voice.

12

RETUNING MY SOUL TO SING GOD'S FREQUENCY WITH THE SONG OF GRATITUDE

Discovering Pain Is My Gift and Tool to Worth, Value, and Voice

G ratitude for the gift of pain releases the sexually abused child, now adult, into freedom for growth to become who God created her to be. Who am I? is the question that plagues every person who has suffered abuse in any degree or in any form whether it be physical, sexual, mental, emotional, verbal, or spiritual. Prolonged abuse, especially, will swallow up the child's identity as she allows others to define who she is.

She has a very long recovery journey ahead of her. She has lived her life in survival mode. And now that she has allowed her husband entrance into her deepest pain, she discovers this pain has opened a deep chasm of raw festering scar tissue. Everyday life causes her to flinch if anyone or anything reminds her of the past wounds which she thought would automatically be healed by ignoring the pain. How is she ever going to clean out the putrid, gangrenous, festering wounds that were scarred over. Scraping off the scar tissue and cleaning out raw pain was going to be excruciatingly painful. She has avoided this kind of pain. She had tried different kinds of "band-aides," "salves," and "balms" that promised five easy steps explaining how to get rid of pain and move on in life. But nothing was working. Her inner core issues were never addressed using these surface methods to relieve her pain. *These quick remedies never told her she would need to embrace the pain and the emotions attached to every trauma that she had kept buried.*

She had many books that lined her library shelves. She had studied much. She had searched for years to find the keys to the healing path that was for her. Talk therapy only seemed to take her to a level that increased her fear, anxiety, depression, and frustration which all increased her rage, shame, blame, guilt, and pain.

What was causing her disconnect? Why could she *not* find answers to this deep emotional distress? Where was God? Why could she *not* see God in all this pain? Why was God such a distant, cold-hearted, nameless, faceless Being who turned His back on her pleas for help? Did her past have anything to do with how she viewed God? Was this part of her inability to trust God or men—not even her husband, the man she deeply loved?

I have been sharing stories about my heart gardens. I want you, my readers, to understand how abuse deeply affects the soul of a child. The distortions that take place are deep in the mind and soul of the child. It takes a lifetime to sort out this entanglement. It is only through perseverance and daily choosing that this child, now adult, slowly replaces the broken and tangled mess with new thought patterns.

When the victim of abuse seems to come to a standstill, makes no progress, shuts down, or resists making deep emotional changes by taking responsibility for their own healing journey, they most likely have reached the bottom of their abysmal pit and are face to face with their haunting questions—Who *is* God to me? Where *was* God when bad things happened? Why did God *not* help or protect me?

I have another difficult story to write. I do not tell you these word-picture stories to hurt others. So many times, the very same people who have acted out abusive behaviors on innocent children, at some point in their long ago forever moment, were the recipients of the exact actions from their own perpetrators. They have not yet dealt with their own painful issues. They do these things because they are still very angry at God. That is our bottom issue. *We resist connecting to God because love was distorted, and we equate God with our perpetrators. It is humiliating to ask the God we hate to forgive us for hating Him.*

How am I, the woman, in this story, going to retune the soul of the abused child in me to sing the frequency of God with *The Song of Gratitude?* I believe you will understand and learn to sing *The Song of Gratitude* with us as you walk through the next garden—*The Garden of the Faceless Man.* We are going to watch the Creator Gardener work His masterpiece of exquisite beauty in this inner core Soul Garden as He transforms it, reclaims it, and renames it to—The Garden of the Song of Gratitude—and here we shall "see" the Face of God!

The Faceless Man no longer controls her inner garden. He left. He could not sing *The Song of Gratitude* with the frequency of God.

The Garden of the Faceless Man, Transformed, Reclaimed, Renamed—The Garden of the Song of Gratitude!

The garden gate into the Inner Core Garden stood ajar again! She was positive that she had closed and locked it as best she could the night before. The rusty corroded hinges made the gate sag, and the lock had a latch that was hard to secure because it was rusty as well. She had not wanted any intruders to gain access to the painful cleanup process she was sorting through. Hmm! How did that gate get open again?

An uncomfortable uneasiness came over her. It just felt like someone had been there in her garden recently. Was it him again? Why won't he leave me alone? Hasn't he already done enough damage? Why does he have to plague my dreams and thoughts? He pops in and out at will whenever he wants to. He never asks permission. He comes and goes as if he owns this garden! He does not! It's MINE!

Why won't he get out and stay out? He always leaves a taint in my mind—like a stain that is permanent. I cannot wash him out of my mind no matter what detergent, stain remover, degreaser, goo gone, gojo, you name it—nothing removes the stain he left deep in my mind. I am so tired of cleaning up the messes he leaves behind. He gets me to do his dirty work and then uses my inner heart garden for his resting place. He smashes everything apart that I try to fix and make beautiful again.

She sat down on the bank of the trickling creek running through her garden. Sadly, she sat looking at the debris littering and clogging up the Spring of Life that used to bubble out joy and peace flowing like a river through her soul. She shook her head in dismay wondering out loud how she had ever allowed all this negative thinking trash to take up root in her mind. Was it because her boundaries had been violated at such a young age? Boundaries. What were boundaries? She would set up wobbly perimeters to keep intruders out, but they were like tiny broken toothpicks lined up to hold back an army of brutal giants.

Why couldn't she set the boundaries in her mind in ways that would block him out forever? She thought she had buried the memories he left behind. Buried deep.

Then, she had invited her husband to look into this garden with her. Her Inner Core—Soul Garden. Now, it seemed everything she had worked so hard to make beautiful for 19 years had taken on a different atmosphere. There was a dismal haze that hung over the whole garden. Nothing would grow with no sunshine to lift her spirits. And, she had always made her own sunshine on cloudy dreary days. She had a happy face mask she always pulled out on those days. That mask was not working for her.

Masks. Faces. Why had she worn so many different faces? Why had she picked up every mask someone else pointed to that belonged to them, and with no resistance she had put their mask on! Not only did she put their mask on! she had acted out their guilt, shame, blame, rage, and pain!

Why?

Oh! That Faceless Man! Why can I *not* get away from him? He takes up my thoughts. He controls my thoughts, and he is not even around. Yet, he is always beside me, in front of me, behind me, over me, under me. In me—Faceless. Faceless masks. A man with no face. Faceless. Nameless. Taking up space, filling up space, in my mind—sucking the life from my soul in the gaping bleeding holes he left in my heart. My Heart—Soul Garden.

Wait! I did know who he was! He was not faceless! I did know his name! He was not nameless! It ripped my soul wide to be open to this kind of pain! Oh! The shame! Why did I have to bear the blame?

Soul Garden. The Soul of a Child. Words pounding within. What was this? She ran to the nook in her Soul Garden where she kept her journal and tools. Grabbing a pencil and the journal, she sat down on the bench that overlooked the creek and flower gardens. Quietly, she sat pondering. Musing. Her heart was beating with a strange knocking. Words. Words. Speaking. *Echoing Silence*. Words. Knocking.

The pent-up dam of words burst from the clogged Spring of Love in her soul—The Soul of the Child was speaking! Nothing could stop the torrent of words that flowed from her fingers as the pencil flew across the pages of her journal.

Tears streaming down her face, she spelled out the agony of her soul in words. Words that spelled out Gratitude for Pain. Words that spelled out her value! Her worth! Words that broke the *Echoing Silence from the Child Within* and gave her voice. Her soul began to sing. She was singing a different frequency! She was Shari—Song of God! Singing in harmony with God, the Song of Gratitude!

She was not just a survivor of sexual abuse! She was overcoming and victorious as she accepted God's view of her! He named her. He valued her! He gave her the key to recovery and showed her how to use acceptance of pain as her gift from Him. He was the One who was doing the surgery, cleaning out the putrid raw cancerous festering wound. He would bind Himself into the open bleeding wounds of her hemorrhaging soul. He would fill the aching void with Himself—His love—for God is love. He would show her how to transform her Soul Garden. He would never leave her or forsake her!

She could accept who she was as God saw her as undamaged, unbroken, and unblemished, the way God values her. He saw her as authentic, virtuous, and vivacious. And, she was His child! She was created by Him to glorify, worship, and love Him as her own Heavenly Father.

Her gift of pain caused her to mine out, excavate, her hidden treasure of tenacity—she had never let go of who she was created to be. By embracing the pain of her broken messy and being grateful for the pain, she steps from darkness to light, from prison to freedom, from silence to sing in harmony with God's frequency. This harmony brings her into fullness of joy. She is Shari—*Song of God.*

And so, she wrote her story in poem form to summarize the past and look into the future of her healing journey. As of today, she is still working out parts of this poem—her Song of God. It has no end until she steps over into another world and bows at His feet and sings a new song of gratitude for His mercy, love, and grace.

As you read through her poem entitled *The Soul of a Child*, think about her journey, and think about your journey. Stop often as you read and journal anything that pops up for you. I have let you know already that this book is not written as a novel to race through and find out what happens at the end. This is written to draw you to the Father of Light. He knows your pain. He loves you and cares about you. And, I love you enough to open my heart—*The Soul of a Child*.

The Soul of a Child

The soul of a child is like a garden so fair,
But the weight of abuse fills the heart with despair.
Fettered with secrets and locked up in fear,
Wounded hearts draw away from those who are near.
Pain like a vice has snuffed out the light,
There is no hope for the wrong to be right.

A pure little girl stood fearful and shamed,
Her virtue was stolen, and it left her ashamed.
Disgrace like a shroud came over her soul,
Confused by the guilt that did over her roll.
Robbed of her virtue her price valued worthless,
Vile men wronged a child so small and so helpless.

Her heart became filled with a dreadful fear,
No one would love her if she shed even a tear.
They threatened with things terrible if ever she told,
Her right to a carefree childhood forever they sold.
She hid for protection behind a thick wall,
For there she was safe from men one and all.

How quickly she left her childhood behind,
For sexual abuse leaves its stain deep in the mind.
The past and its memories hauntingly call,
The only relief was to bury it all.
The smile that she wore was happy and bright,
But the person inside had gone out like a light.

Living but dead she struggled to live,
The question before her was, "Can Jesus forgive?"
Brokenhearted she cried in her room all alone,
"Oh, Jesus, for this sin does your blood yet atone?"
Was it her sin? Was it for this that she prayed?
Is this how Jesus felt when He was betrayed?

Desires of vile men made deep wounds in her heart,
For sexual abuse leaves scars from its poisonous dart.
Have they no care for the soul left with a blight?
To see her frantic terror is that what gave them delight?
Do they still hear the anguished cry that reached all heaven?
Can men so wicked and vile be yet forgiven?

For men she had such a loathing aversion,
And before God she felt viewed as abomination.
Crushed and broken, abuse had wounded her heart.
For the innocent victim can there be a new start?
All men were scorned with seething distrust,
Up in Heaven was there really a God who is Just?

Into her life God sent a stalwart young man,
His love won her heart for God had a plan.
So tender and kind was the man she had found,
No walls did she need when he was around!
Their love was like flowers that bloom in the Spring,
Her heart was so happy for in the night it could sing!

No fear did she have when he asked for her hand,
For her thoughts were not on what all God had planned.
She buried the past and entered marital bliss,
She thought that her wounds needed only his kiss.
Deep within memory stirred like restless waves of the sea,
It was the soul of a child crying to be free.

She was a woman now, a blighted rose in full bloom,
The past with its shame kept her spirit bound up in gloom.
Must all her life be spent chained up in fear?
"Oh, God," was her cry, "I cannot shed even a tear!"
Her heart was cleansed, she knew freedom from sin,
But the deeds of vile men had wrought havoc within.

Was not the love of a Savior and husband enough?
What was this hardness that made her seem tough?
What was the restless longing that stirred deep within?
Why did emotions demand she obey every whim?
Why did the past call from deep in the grave?
Emotions controlled her and made her their slave.

The cry of her soul God heard from on high,
as she embraced the emotions she had tried to deny.
She would feel soul pain as if it were a red-hot brand,
The wound He would heal with the imprint of His
own hand.
Line upon line the finger of God brought her deep pain,
Embrace her emotions? How could that bring her gain?

Her life was a vessel, but it was made with a flaw,
How crippled and useless was what the Potter saw.
He then took of the clay a new vessel to make,
With deep sorrow her soul He would have to shake.
How tender His love as His arms drew her near!
For He must touch the one to her heart most dear.

121

Tragedy struck with a heart-rending blow,
Like torrents of rain in her heart tears did flow.
Her husband was brought home, but he was not the same.
"Oh, God," was her cry, "I don't know why this sorrow came."
Her heart was broken, and she wanted to cry,
"Oh, why? For what reason did a man have to die?"

Sorrow stabbed through like the thrust of a knife,
Her husband lay so ill, she despaired of his life.
The days were so long but even darker the night,
Faith now was tested, "Why don't you give up the fight?"
The Father then saw that all love He must sever,
She did not want to place trust in God or a man ever!

The Savior was there, but He hid from her view,
Her faith must be strengthened, the light He withheld too.
The giant of fear attacked with all his might,
"Oh, God, are You there?" was her cry in the night.
The darkness was real, no light could she see,
In panic she ran, then stumbled and fell to her knees.

"Oh, Jesus, please help me or else I will perish,
I surrender to You all the things that I cherish.
Take all my plans and wishes, I want only Your will.
Teach me quietness and how to be still.
Help me!—I know not how to trust God.
Jesus, please show me the path that You have trod."

Her prayers were but sobs and then only a moan,
She went to her Gethsemane and entered alone.
Her questions would be stilled as she prayed in agony,
She would learn to deny self for yonder was Calvary.
To give forth fragrance the blighted rose would be crushed.
Only with bitter grief would all her soul be hushed.

How gently the Savior lead through the Valley of Tears,
    She confessed to her husband all her fears.
Through the anguish and sorrow, his love held her up,
    To accept grief as a gift was to drink the bitter cup.
Terror swept over her soul as the blackest of night.
    "Oh, God, are You there? Will I ever find Light?"

With trembling and fear she told of the past,
    "You lie, you lie," was Satan's terrible blast.
But something inside began to sing a glad song,
    "I am going to be free, oh, Jesus, to You I belong.
Chains of fear bind me around, all the truth I will tell,
    I am afraid now to hide, I want out of my shell!"

All hell then broke loose, for her soul they would fight,
    The LORD himself came near and flooded her with Light.
She knew the faceless man had to be given his name,
    It ripped her soul wide to be open to shame.
The soul of the child now writhed in her fear,
    "Oh! What will I do if ever he should hear?"

Many more men were each given his name,
    The guilt was not hers; they all were to blame.
The truth she did tell, she could look at each face,
    Strength to forgive was hers because of God's grace.
"Father, forgive them, they know not what they do,
    The past I could forget if they only knew You."

O blessed sorrow that makes the wounded whole,
    Such was the path of healing for her wounded soul.
From the prison of pain her soul found release,
    For in acceptance therein lieth sweet peace.
It was from God's hand that all had transpired,
    To tell of His mercy she would never be tired.

All love was transformed that her soul might be free,
Renewing her mind, bringing her thoughts into captivity.
The battles are fought, and the victories won,
The cry of a child is hushed for the work is all done.
A virtuous woman she is with a heart full of Light!
Her wounds are healed by the power of His might!

The Valley of Sorrow was a beautiful place,
For Jesus was there to give God's riches of grace.
Perfumed flowers of gentleness and mercy she'd find,
Treasures of patience that taught her to be kind.
Compassion and longsuffering shone as spun gold,
How tender His Love her wounded heart to enfold.

The Valley of Tears was shadowed by grief and pain,
But joy came in the morning like sunshine after rain.
Weeping endured only for the long dark night,
With acceptance of pain there dawned glorious Light!
The suffering and pain had been working for good,
The grief and sorrow she now understood.

Suffering and pain have consumed all the dross,
What glorious victory to glory in the cross!
Why should her soul in grief repine?
What joy to be counted worthy her gold to refine!
Suffering was perfected for sorrow is sweet delight,
Walking with Jesus every burden is light!

The Spring of Love now all her heart does consume,
Out of it, fragrant flowers grow of Eternal bloom.
Her heart is as soft as ground plowed in the Spring,
The seed has sprung forth, good fruit it will bring.
Love ever new comes from the Father she trusts.
Sorrows and joys are from the hand of a God who's just.

A glad happy song now within her soul sings,
Bubbling and laughing it flows like a spring.
Her heart is a garden with flowers so fair,
Her price is above rubies, she is valued as rare!
The fingers of God left such beautiful scars,
Bowed at His feet songs of praise rise past the stars.

Her heart is so happy for she walks in the Light!
For Truth she hungers, all wrong to be right.
No longer a flower with a blight on her soul,
Beautiful rose in full bloom by the Creator Gardener made
whole.
Transformed by His hand fragrant perfume fills the air,
Bowed at His feet for the sexually abused she pleads now in
prayer.

© Shari Rickenbach, November 28, 1995

PART 4

REALIGNING IN GOD'S CREATIVE DESIGN

The journey to this point has been tough, facing challenges we never knew we would have to confront because we chose to find our healing path to wholeness. Until now we have been doing surgery and cleaning out daily the cancerous roots of abuse. We feel raw, exposed, vulnerable, emotionally drained, and yet there is a new pulsating, throbbing sense of life springing up from deep within. Hope has ignited and fanned the flickering, smoldering ruin to a blaze that begins to burn the dross left from the residue of abuse. Learning to hold still in the Refiner's fire is our process to progress.

We are looking for the gold hidden deep within where we buried the treasure of our true identity. This is where we truly find our identity in Christ. We co-create with God by finding His beauty hidden in us. We reflect His beauty in broken messy. We use our setbacks to become our comebacks by relentless agreement and repetitive forgiveness. And best of all, we finally discover our Heavenly Father has never demanded perfection from us. He has been waiting with open arms to love us because—God is Love—God is Good—All the Time.

13

RECREATING TO CO-CREATE GOD'S BEAUTY IN ME

Overcoming with My O.A.R. to Be a Victor

Who is God to me? What is Truth? How have I allowed my belief systems to be tainted with the victim mentality? Have I projected these twisted, skewed perceptions formed in childhood to coincide with a false identity? Will I continue to believe God's love is equal to the ideas and thought patterns embedded in my mind by evil men of what love means and project this on God?

These are the questions the sexually abused child, now woman, must apply to every area of her life. This is to confront and wage war with the enemy of her soul. This is a battle between God and Satan. What will she choose this time? Truth or Lies?

To choose Truth is to pick up her O.A.R. and become a Victor and Overcomer. She must daily pick up her O.A.R. as her weapon of defense. She is confronting and overcoming her victim B.E.D. Her lifelong victim B.E.D. of Blame. Excuses. Denial. She is setting fire to her B.E.D. She is refusing to call it her comfort zone. She is doing this by taking Ownership, being Accountable, and taking Responsibility for her own actions. She is in the trenches engaging in soul warfare doing the messy work of sorting through broken.

She is in the depths of her abyss co-creating with God. She is alone, but not alone. The Father who thought of her before she was born is right there with her. And in her dark night of the soul, she finds God. She finds beauty in broken messy. She finds her identity in Christ.

The Neglected Forget-Me-Not Garden

Gardens speak her soul language. Working in her flower gardens barefooted, she wonders if this is how Adam and Eve felt as they walked and talked with God. Did they find it was easy to commune with God and tell Him their soul secrets?

God seemed closer when she was kneeling in the damp earthy loam, her flowers nodding their heads in the breeze as if they too were singing their love song to their Creator. She noticed that even the shy little violets peeking out from under the rosebushes were smiling their joyful praise. All creation was breathing and pulsating with joy. The birds flitted here and there filling the airwaves with the frequency of joy. What was this expectancy that was drawing her wounded heart into stillness and quietness? The birds felt it too and hushed their singing. The flowers held their faces to a beam of light that moved across the garden warming it with love light.

She waited, too. Quietly, the Master Creator Gardener sat on the grass beside her. Quietness and stillness continued to fill the aching void in her soul. Her heart drank in new strength and confidence as they discussed the different areas her gardens were growing with renewed vigor. He complemented her efforts to change her ways of thinking negatively and showed her how by choosing this simple remedy, her garden was bearing the fruits of restoration. Broken plants that needed special care were responding to gentleness. The Master Gardener drew her attention to some beautiful plants that were blooming profusely and filling the garden with perfumed fragrance. The smell was so heavenly they got up and walked over to see which ones were giving them such delight.

They were her flowers of relentless forgiveness and unconditional love. He pointed out that these had been abundantly watered with her tears of acceptance with joy. Right in the middle of experiencing extreme pain as she pruned off the broken bedraggled stems and dead flowers, she was learning that the pain she was feeling in the moment was her gift. It was her priceless gift—the antidote to shame, blame, guilt, rage, fear, and pain. The antidote that nourished the root system of her soul. Her roots had tapped into the River of Life Eternal!

They sat again in silence for a while, and then, the Creator Gardener nodded toward a corner of her garden that was overgrown with weeds. She really did not want to explore that part of the garden. It had been a beautiful little nook full of forget-me-nots. These were a special variety that grew nowhere except in her soul. These forget-me-nots grew out of the essence of who she really was. The Creator had planted those flowers Himself. They were the fruits of who He had created her to be. Each fruit had a different character trait that was uniquely her.

Grace was her secret name. Her Creator had given her that name before she was born. He knew her. Taking her by the hand, the Master Gardener walked with her over to the ugly corner of her heart garden. This was the next section of recovery she was going to be working on. The task before her was overwhelming—until she looked into the Gardener's eyes. His eyes were full of love—He was not seeing her as broken and messy—He was seeing her as His own created being, living out His purpose, His why, His reason for creating her. He was pleased with who she was becoming.

He saw all the obstacles and deep dark valleys she would be passing through. He knew that she would be using fear as her fuel to overcome the habits and learned behaviors that would threaten to drag her back into a negative destructive lifestyle.

He saw she would face great oppositions that already had well laid plans to destroy her—the person she was created to be. There would be close acquaintances who would bully, threaten, block, thwart and frustrate her choices to change and to realign in God's creative design for her.

And God saw her. And God smiled.

He did not promise her an easy recovery road to travel. He did not tell her she would not have a painless process. He did not tell her about the smothering soul darkness she would live with for years. He did not show her how to avoid the heartbreak of broken relationships and betrayals. He did not reveal that she was set on a journey leading through the deepest darkest abysmal pit she had ever encountered, and she would have no words to describe her terror.

But He did whisper these words, "Be still and know I am God." "In quietness and confidence shall be your strength." "Choose you this day whom you will serve." "I am God, beside Me there is no other." "I will never leave you or forsake you." "I am not a man that I should lie." "I have loved you with an everlasting love." "You are mine. I have redeemed you. I have called you by your name. You are Grace."

The quietness enveloped her soul. She stood looking at the weeds of shame, blame, excuses, denial, fear, rage, guilt, and pain. She was quiet as she contemplated what had to be done. She had no ideas or ready plans how to clean up the mess she had made by her negligence. She feared what would happen if she uncovered all her buried emotions that were attached to the painful memories. But, was the pain of remaining frozen and stuck in fear worth choosing to continue living life dead?

She *thought* about the consequences of living life dead in toxic fear. She *felt* those buried emotions. She embraced the painful memories connected to each emotion. And then, she turned away from living life dead—she *chose*! *She chose—Life!* *She had two choices—Life or Death!*

She chose—Life! Breathing deeply and freely a smile spread across her face. She had never known such profound peace and joy! *In that moment of deliberate choice, a river of Life Abundant coursed through her being flooding and bursting the dam of frozen Echoing Silence! She came alive! Her whole being was lifted to a higher frequency—the frequency of God!*

And God smiled.

Her triumphant joyous laugh rang out through the Neglected Forget-Me-Not Garden. The birds hushed their singing—her joy was beyond compare! The flowers bowed their heads as she fell at the Master Creator's feet in worship—"My Lord and my God, I worship You in this valley, in this place, in this journey, because You do all things well!"

Again, God smiled.

He was pleased she had found the balm of healing for her wounded broken soul—Worship. Worshiping Him in the midst of the Refiner's flame, learning to be still and quiet while the dross was consumed, the fiery furnace was not meant to destroy her—no, The Creator Refiner was looking for the gold He saw in her.

She did not understand what the Refiner's process was going to feel like. She would need this healing balm of worship throughout her journey. In fact, as she knelt on the hardened soil of the Forget-Me-Not Garden, she wondered how she had ever thought the Victim B.E.D. of *blame, excuses, and denial* was a comfortable place to make her home. Why had she lived there for so many years?

Blame was a tough weed to root out! Excuses were not any easier to remove! They had their tap roots far below the surface, spreading out in all directions like thistles and creeping jenny! She pulled out root after root only to dig deeper and find they were entangled in every cell of her body! How had that happened? Was it possible that living in toxic fear had opened her mind, soul, and body to more destruction than she could imagine?

This was just too much! Better to deny that generational abuse had had an adverse effect on her all her life! Wait! This victim B.E.D. was not her home anymore! What was she thinking? Crazy eight patterns again!

This choosing stuff was hard work! Blood, sweat, and tears kind of work! *Who would have thought choosing would take so much effort and discipline!* Was this pain of changing worth it?

She paused, wiping sweat off her face, and looking at the pile of weeds a slow smile began to twinkle at the corners of her eyes. Ah, yes! Peace and joy flowed like a river within her heart garden making this task seem lighter. The whole garden around her was holding its breath wondering if she was going to finish the job she had started.

Sitting back on her heels, she surveyed the garden, eye to eye with her soul flowers. This was her garden. This was her soul she was looking at.

This was her choice to choose Life. Life would be Life only if she kept choosing Life! Yes! —That's it! —Life! Every moment she would choose Life!

Her garden breathed a sigh a relief. They would live. They could all grow together! She would water each fragile plant with her tears, she would cultivate the soil of her heart with obedience and perseverance. She would nurture every fiber of her being by picking up her new garden tool—her O.A.R.!

You are kidding! Use an O.A.R. in a garden? Where's the lake, river, or ocean? Wait! She *did* say there was a river of peace and joy that was springing up! What is this O.A.R.? It's the O.A.R. of taking Ownership, being Accountable, and taking Responsibility for my own actions.

Getting up off the victim B.E.D., she walks over to her toolbox and picks up the O.A.R. Carrying her O.A.R. back to the Forget-Me-Not Garden, she notices her O.A.R. has shaped itself to a nice sharp surgeon's scalpel!

Denial saw her coming and popped his head out from under the B.E.D. shouting, "I did not do it! I had nothing to do with making this B.E.D.! I am not the one who makes you feel bad! I haven't done one single thing to deserve this treatment! You cannot make me leave!"

Blame tried to run when he heard the shouts of Denial. Yelling at Denial he hurled his insults, "Denial, you bully! You brought us all into this B.E.D. You lied. You made us fill up this B.E.D. with hard rocks and stones of shame, guilt, anger, rage, fear, and every negative thing you could stuff this B.E.D. with. You are the one who causes trouble. You are the one who never wants to change your dirty socks! You make life miserable for everybody. This is your fault she is coming after us! Run! She means business! I do not like the fiery look in her eye! Yikes! She is going to burn this B.E.D.! Oh! Our beautiful hard rocky B.E.D., she won't let us call it home anymore!"

Excuses came prancing off the B.E.D. "Now, now, my Dear! What are you so upset about? We haven't quite got the B.E.D. made yet, but that's because we did not have enough time. Besides, the covers are not long enough, and we do not have money to buy something better and make it more comfortable for you. Plus, we just haven't had the energy to help you get this B.E.D. unstuck from the negative thinking soil in your brain. You really should give up your ideas of making changes to get rid of our B.E.D., because we haven't been able to rent another spot."

Undeterred by the voices of Blame, Excuses, and Denial, she walked with purpose to the victim B.E.D. that was mired in her Forget-Me-Not Garden. Her fortitude was strengthened, and she yanked that B.E.D. out using the O.A.R. as a pry bar. With the Victor's cry ringing out through her garden, she attacked the victim B.E.D. using the O.A.R. as a weapon of war! She took back Ownership! She took over Accountability. Responsibility for her own actions stood saluting, waiting to carry out her orders and quickly make corrections and apologies. Together, they burned her victim B.E.D.!

Strangely, the fire that burned up a formidable foe in her garden, ignited a fire that consumed the dross connecting the entire root system. This was a flame that purified the negative residue from sexual abuse and set her soul on fire! Now, she could advance and make progress in the recovery process with defined purpose, clarity, and confidence as she daily realigned to the design the Master Gardener had created in her!

The Forget-Me-Not Garden looked so different without her victim B.E.D.! The little flowers of joy, pleasure, delight, sweetness, charm, loveliness, mercy, goodness, patience, truthfulness, consideration, generosity, tenderness, compassion, and elegance to name a few had sprung to life. They grew so fast with the sunshine of the Creator Gardener beaming down on them. They were free from the overshadowing B.E.D. that had stunted their growth! They were set free to bless the world with the fragrance of her life lived out to her fullest potential.

The cool of the evening kissed her cheeks as she walked and talked with the Gardener Creator of her Soul Garden. They stood together drinking in the beauty of her Forget-Me-Not Garden. She had fought and won a difficult battle that day. Peace reigned in her Soul Garden. She was at rest. She was moving forward in quietness and confidence. Moving forward and quietly resting at the same time. At peace. At home with herself. Realigned with her Creator the way He had created her to be. Ready to co-create with the Creator of Life.

Come, take a walk with me, and we shall explore the reflections of God's creative image through her broken as she co-creates, and God recreates in her.

14

REFLECTING GOD'S CREATIVE IMAGE

Finding Wholeness in Broken Messy

Nature reveals God's creative power. Since God created the worlds out of nothing, can He not create beauty from the ruin and ash heap of her broken messy? She cannot separate herself from broken messy. She cannot run away from the dark shadows that have pursued her through life.

She will find wholeness when she turns to the Light to embrace all her broken—*every shard!* She must embrace all the broken and allow those shards to pierce deeply into the core of who she has become—accepting this excruciating pain as a gift. In this acceptance of pain, she shall have peace.

The Garden of Broken Shards

The Creator Gardener came early to her garden while the dew hung heavy on the roses. Their blooms, drooping low under the weight of dew from the mist that shrouded the garden in mystery, gave the appearance the roses were weeping. The dew, dripping like tears, washed away the grime encrusted on little bits of something hidden in the flowerbeds. There were glints of reflected light bouncing into the shadows under the many rosebushes. What was causing the light to bounce into the shadows? Where was the reflecting image of Light coming from? How was it being reflected into and through her Soul Garden?

Yesterday, she had cultivated the different flowerbeds while the Creator Gardener taught her of His love and grace and mercy. Their communion had been sweet, and her soul was comforted and nourished. She loved these times with the Creator Gardener. While they talked, she worked diligently, digging up every weed He lovingly pointed to that was not growing in His Heart. She was learning that her heart garden would be a peaceful, beautiful place only if it contained the flowers He had planted in her. His heart had no ugly cancerous weeds. He was making her heart garden look like His.

But she was doing the hard, difficult, uncomfortable, and painful cultivating of her heart garden. No one else could do this for her. He was right there to strengthen, uplift, and dump in oceans of Grace, but her obedience and doing what He showed her step by step, was the antidote to her shame, blame, guilt, fear, and pain she so desperately wanted to be set free from.

Each time she pulled out weeds like irritated, frustrated, resentful, seething, stubborn, ashamed, despairing, hopeless, worthless, faultfinding, fearful, rejected, unloved, shamed, blamed, belittled, guilty, hateful, suspicious, humiliated, dirty, defenseless, tainted, liar, powerless, and negativity to name a few, she felt a surge of new life. She had many questions to ask about each weed as she yanked it from the soil of her heart garden. Holding out His nail-scarred hands, the Gardener took each offensive weed, and then gently, tenderly explained to her how she did not need to hold, ever again, any of the weeds that had been growing in her heart. He was tossing the whole ugly pile into His Sea of Forgiveness, never to remember she had allowed any weed to grow and spoil her inward beauty in the garden He had created.

The Creator Gardener then knelt on the freshly cultivated soil of her Soul Garden. Taking flower seeds from His own heart He began to sow seeds of kindness, gentleness, goodness, long-suffering, patience, tenderness, forgiveness, unconditional love, harmony, peace, joy, compassion, gratitude, delight, graciousness, serenity, trust, virtue, and tranquility.

The soil had been well watered with her tears of repentance, and in the sunshine of the Creator Gardener's love, the seeds quickly sprouted and began growing the most gorgeous plants she had ever seen! What would the flowers look like? She asked Him how soon she would see the fruits of His planting. Smiling, He looked deep into her eyes for a long moment. Satisfied with what He saw in her, He nodded.

"Grace," He said gently, "I am not going to let you see the flowers or their fruits. The flowers are not yours to enjoy just yet. When I present you to our Heavenly Father, then you will see the fruits of righteousness that I have planted in your heart garden. For right now, I am entrusting you to care for and cultivate what I put in you to live out for my honor and glory. I am a very jealous God. You may have all of who I AM. I AM everything you will ever need. I fill every void. I AM Love. I AM your God. I AM your Lord and Savior. My Father is your Father. He is the Father of Light and in Him there is no shadow of turning.

"Come, Grace, I have something to show you that's hidden under the rosebushes."

They walked toward the roses following the winding paths through the many beautiful gardens she had been cultivating. There was a twinkling and glimmering shine all around the plants she had spent so much time on recently. What was it? She hadn't noticed it yesterday. Maybe she hadn't been able to see because her eyes had poured out gallons and gallons of tears as she worked. She remembered her fingers had been touching something broken—almost like pieces of how she felt—Broken. Maybe she should ask her Creator Gardener to put her back together—all those bits of pieces of who she used to be—maybe He could fix her broken so that no one would ever be able to see her flaws and ugly cracks of pain.

Nearing the Rose Gardens, the Gardener hummed a happy song. She found her soul responding with joy, and soon she was humming in harmony with Him. Her soul was tuned to a different new frequency! The roses smiled their glad welcome and their delightful perfume filled the air. Under the rosebushes she noticed a different sort of shine was being reflected from a glowing depth that warmed her soul. She felt loved. The dewdrops still hung like tears from the morning mist and dripped on the glow increasing the love she felt. What was this?

Then, she remembered the bits and pieces she wanted the Creator to fix. Turning to Him, a deep yearning for wholeness gripping her soul, she spoke in a low tearful voice, choking over the lump in her throat, "When I was cultivating yesterday, I found hundreds of millions of tiny pieces that were me. Can you fix me—take all those pieces and put me back together so that no one will see how broken I've been?"

"Shari, Song of God, I am going to do above all that you ask or think! I am going to shine from all this broken in you. My Child, you are Mine! This, that is broken in you, is part of who you are. I will be glorified in this broken. I am shining from every broken shard to bless the broken around you. I was broken for you on the cross. I use broken. I find you altogether lovely because I AM Altogether Lovely in you—*in this broken.* Wholeness is found in the mind of Christ, in Me, your Redeemer. And you are renewed, made into My likeness, as you bring your thoughts into captivity by renewing your mind in Me, Christ."

"I AM the Rose of Sharon. I AM the Lily of the Valley. I AM the Bright and Morning Star. I have given you the secret name of Grace for a reason. My Grace is sufficient for you. Do you see the shine, the depth of glow all through this Rose Garden? This glow is coming from the depths of deep soul suffering. I walked with you through the Valley of Sorrow and The Valley of Tears. Those tears you have shed have not been forgotten. I bottled up those tears of sorrow and suffering."

"Grace, the depth of the shine that you see under the roses is the reflected light from your tears that you have shed in the darkness of the valleys you have walked through, are walking through, and will walk through. Those hot scalding tears were not wasted, nor will they be wasted. Those are the tears that are being poured out in the prayers I pray through you for broken humanity."

"Grace, your heart garden is My temple where I live and move and have My being. And you live and move and have your being in Me. In Christ Jesus, Me, you have your reason, your purpose, your why. I created you. Your true identity is in Me. In Christ. In Me you have Life—Life Abundant in purity, restoration, and hope. I Am your Lord and God. God Himself reflects His creative image through your broken to re-create and co-create with you. You are no longer co-dependent, but you are co-creator with the Creator Himself."

She had a choice now. The Creator Gardener had given her an answer to the questions that plagued her mind. She wanted wholeness of mind, body, and soul, but His answer was not at all what she expected. If He had created her, her anticipation was that He would instantly put her pieces together exactly like she had been so many years ago.

She thought. She pondered. She reflected. She understood. She chose.

She chose to embrace all the broken as part of who she is right now. She chose to allow all the broken to pierce deeply into her core being of who she has become. She chose to accept this excruciating pain as a gift. In this acceptance of pain, she moved through the pain into Peace. Abiding Peace.

Peace that passes all understanding. Peace of mind, body, and soul. Peace that stilled the raging within. Peace—the Prince of Peace, the Creator Gardener Himself, had taken up residence in her Soul Garden.

Now that the Prince of Peace resides in her Soul Garden everything is a beautiful perfect summer day, right? Wrong. She is ready to co-create with God doing even more difficult inner work. She will have lots of setbacks. However, she is going to do something completely different! She will use those setbacks to be her comebacks.

Come, I will show you another garden she is cultivating as she begins Restoring Relationships by Relentless Agreement and Repetitive Forgiveness. The Marriage Garden leads into the Four Small Heart Gardens.

15

RESTORING RELATIONSHIPS BY RELENTLESS AGREEMENT AND REPETITIVE FORGIVENESS

Co-creating with God Using Setbacks to Be Comebacks

Perhaps this stage of recovery from sexual trauma is the most deciding factor in the development of new habits and mindsets that change learned behaviors. The Victor—Overcomer of sexual trauma does well, makes great changes, and then she finds herself feeling like she is back at square one, back in the same pit, on the same crazy eight. Why? How? Where does she go from here? What triggered her responses? Who is responsible when circumstances blow her out of the water? *Choices. Her choices.*

Turning *setbacks to comebacks* is hard, daily, difficult inner work. Setbacks are not failures. Setbacks are the opportunities life offers to reassess, to readjust, to realign her inner core. Setbacks are her gifts to open and look at the person she is becoming as she recreates and co-creates with God. Her setbacks are her comebacks as she puts into practice her relentless agreement to co-create with God.

Probably one of the greatest setbacks in the recovery journey are the triggers that seem to pop out of nowhere and shake her foundational core being. She has just had a wonderful moment as she grasps ahold of some new truth and makes a massive change in her thinking patterns. She may have been working diligently in this new area of recovery for several weeks, even months, or it could have been just a few hours. She is starting to do life better, and there is a sense of satisfaction in accomplishing something very difficult.

She is in the middle of great rejoicing. Then, BOOM! BAM! She had a trigger pulled, and she was suddenly blown out of the water! What happened! She is knocked for a loop and as usual, she loses her equilibrium for a while. This can cause her much emotional pain, and she may be thrown back into her cycles of depression, anxiety, or discouragement.

She does not understand what just happened. What does she do now? *Choice, again, is her key. Either she chooses to embrace the old thought patterns and behaviors of habit, or she pauses long enough to be able to step back from the painful situation or circumstance she just encountered. This pause helps her to reassess, to readjust, to re-conceptualize, and continue to make the choices that help her to realign to who God made her to be. This propels her forward in her journey to wholeness.*

Does she have to do all this messy work perfectly? No! Have you ever had a wound that became infected? It was very sore at first, and then there was a redness that developed. If you did not take care of the wound and get it cleaned out, the redness turned fiery, not only in color but pain as well. Then pus formed. What next? That infection had to be taken care of! That wound had to go through a deep cleaning process that was very painful. It took time to heal. It required special attention and care. Right?

Why do we think the wounding to our emotional well-being is something to be taken lightly? This wounding affects us mind, body, and soul. It's become infected. The infection has permeated our whole being. It's like a cancerous wound that's full of pus poisoning every aspect of life. Why is it so easy to

glibly tell the abused person to just forgive, forget, and move
on in life? Or worse, tell her she has some unconfessed sin,
or that she is beyond hope? Why do we inflict more pain in
the soul of the person who is barely functioning in life? She
can barely hold her head up. She may not even be able to
look you in the eye. She is struggling to make it from one
day to the next.

She is trying so hard to make a comeback. She just had
a huge setback. Maybe she is looking to you to give her that
loving word of encouragement. Maybe she just needs a shoulder
to cry on while she tries again to sort through broken messy.
She has a tough job to do. Remember, it was not her choice
that she ended up a broken mess. She was an innocent child
at one time. She had no one to guide her to find her recovery
path when she was young. She had years, layers of pain to
work through.

She is doing her best to take responsibility for her own
actions. She is being accountable. She is taking ownership for
her own healing journey. Picking up her O.A.R. and rowing
her boat upstream is hard difficult exhausting work. She is
drained physically, mentally, spiritually, emotionally, and she
just had another setback! She needs a huge space of Grace
where she can rest and regain her equilibrium!

What if you gave her the gift of time alone, quiet space?
Is she a young mother? What if you lifted her heavy load for
a few hours? Oh, you are not doing this to find out about all
her faults and failures adding fresh juicy gossip to the social
media grist mill. No, this is true love poured out, coming
alongside a suffering soul who at the moment needs the hands
of God in human form to reach out and touch her, giving her
a reason to press on through her deep dark valley. What if in
some way you could lighten her darkness and show her there
is hope! There is healing! There is Light!

Her healing journey to wholeness leads through deep
dark valleys. The darkness is smothering. There is a terror

indescribable that grips her soul as she goes to confront fear in the place her soul died. It takes time and energy to return to the pain we have desperately tried to run away from. It pursues us like the shadow of ourselves that we can never get away from.

We cannot get away. It's part of who we are. Those pieces are part of the whole. We never find wholeness until we turn around and embrace the worst part of us. That part is the answer we search for. It's our ugly hard thing that we flee from and is exactly what we must embrace and accept as ours. Pain. We will do anything to avoid this kind of pain.

Pain. That haunting pain that engulfs and smothers trying to snuff life out of us. Pain that clings, nagging constantly, reminding us of the broken—all that we desperately want to put together. Pain that permeates, tainting our thoughts, words, and actions. Pain that reminds us of how we grew up, and we vow to never reproduce this pain in our offspring—but we do. Why? We never allowed the silenced Child Within to have her voice.

Pain. We watch our children grow into maturity shackled with our pain. We did not plan on this. We tried to do life differently. How did it happen? Moment by moment. What now?

Pain. I open my soul for you to see pain. We have already walked through the Marriage Garden—But that garden did not end there. It continued into another garden area. This garden was one I tended very carefully, lavishing much time here as I cultivated Four Small Heart Gardens. I did not have a book entitled *Manual for Broken Mothers on How to Grow Small Heart Gardens.* I just had a heart full of broken love to pour out. It was not enough—but it was my *best.*

Four Small Heart Gardens

She had cultivated and slowly transformed the many flower gardens in her Soul Garden. She had recreated the different gardens into breathtaking beauty. The little arbor nooks with benches, fountains, stone walkways led to grassy resting places beside the Spring of Joy that bubbled out peace, calmness, and serenity creating an atmosphere of quiet, restful, tranquility. Her soul was at rest with who the Creator Gardener had created her to be. She had found, at last, her identity in Christ. The aching void of her deep soul need was filled. Quiet joyful tranquility reigned from the core center of her being. At home. Safe with who she was created to be.

Hidden here and there among the rose gardens there were four special little heart gardens tucked tightly into the essence of who she was. Actually, there had been five gardens. One garden was so tiny that God transplanted her ahead of time into His own little Joy Garden. She had carried the other four gardens nestled close under her heart for nine months, thrilling with the joy of new life kicking, pummeling, turning, active in their growth as they anticipated the moment when they would birth themselves with their own identities, each one different as could be, but all created by God.

She loved those little gardens, and in her every waking moment she guarded them with the fierceness of a mother bear—protecting, ever watchful, vigilant lest the same kind of abuse would destroy her treasures, her gifts from God. In the night hours, her mother heart was tuned to hear their slightest whimper, leaving her warm bed to gather them close, nurturing and lulling them to sleep again. The long nights of restless sickness were no sacrifice for her exhausted body. She watched through the hours of fevered anxiousness until the break of dawn, rejoicing in the morning light that her little garden was resting in healing sleep.

She taught her little heart gardens about Jesus and His love for them. She wanted the best for each garden and taught them that giving was better than receiving. She read many character- building stories to them. Bedtime was a special ending of the day to make certain that each garden felt safe and reassured. No matter what had happened today, tomorrow would be a new day, a fresh new start. Forgiveness was the bedtime seal of a kiss on each little forehead.

She did not understand the growing terror that plagued her mind as she watched her little gardens developing, moving through all the delightful stages. Birthdays were poignant milestones, and each year the little gardens excitedly looked through her cake decorating books to find their special cake— just for their moment, just for them, as they opened the door to another number counting up.

She wanted to do the things for them she had been denied. She wanted her little heart gardens to have childhood.

Only, she did not know how to show them what childhood was like. It was not there in her memory bank. She read stories to them to give them understanding. She tried to play the fun games of childhood, but she could not remember them. She came up empty. The balls and board games were difficult to connect with. All she remembered was a teddy bear at some point, some dolls and a bike. Those had been removed. She felt detached as she watched her husband having fun with their little gardens. Their laughter rang out in childish glee as they chased the soccer ball with dad. She loved watching—but she could not connect.

She taught them good things. She showed them how to work—working alongside, together, laughing, and enjoying doing daily tasks together. But that was really all she knew— work. She never stopped to rest, really enjoy her baby gardens. Oh, she cared for them. Made sure they were fed, dressed in fresh clean clothes, always bathed, and smelling of shampoo, soaps, and lotions. She ironed all their clothes. Yes, they looked good on the outside, but she could not reach the inside where they needed her the most for their sense of safety and

security. She could tend to the physical needs, but the void
of her own emotional health—mind, body, soul connection
was disconnected in their formative years.

She tried to guide them on a spiritual path by teaching
them that Jesus loved them, gave Himself for them on the
cross. She could not explain to them that God was their
Father, and that God is Love because she herself was disconnected from God the Father. To her, He was a rigid austere
Being who was watching and waiting to punish her for every
mistake. She tried to talk about the Love of God, she taught
them songs, and read Bible stories, taught them to pray, told
them what they should do, but she could not live out what
she was teaching—it was not connected because she was
not connected to the source of Life, to the Father of Light.
Paradox. How could she love Jesus and hate God at the same
time? In reality, her inner core disconnect was passed to her
four small heart gardens.

Confusion reigned. Confusion repels. Bright sunshiny laughter bubbled from her lips, but the windows of her soul spoke a
different language and frequency from her eyes. Her little gardens were reading her eyes—not her lips. Her hands were gentle,
hugging, comforting them in their childish sorrows—her spirit
was detached holding them at arm's length. Loving them—but
inadvertently causing deep pain and hurt, thinking that she was
protecting them, doing things different and better—but daily
sowing the seeds of generational brokenness.

How was it she was so blinded? If her soul were seeking
deeper higher values of truth, how did she go so far astray
in believing that God did not, could not love her until she
proved herself good enough? She was acting out exactly what
she had been programmed to believe when her heart garden
was small. She had learned how to detach herself from pain,
remember? In that detachment, she automatically inflicted
the same pain on her little heart gardens the exact same way
she had been wounded.

She did do something different than the generations before. She found repetitive forgiveness grew out of the soil of repentance watered with many tears. Humility sweetened the bitterness of humiliation that she had done the same to those she loved more than life. How could she stop causing this pain to her treasures? How could she put an end to generational abuse? What could she do to stop this gigantic machine that had rolled through to more generations? She had already sowed the same sort of seeds—different variety, different hybrids. Her four small heart gardens perhaps could withstand the storms of life—maybe! But, maybe not.

Overcome with grief and sorrow she gathered the memories of her four small heart gardens into the depths of her soul—holding *Echoing Silence*. She sat weeping! Brokenness! How could she fix this horrible broken messy when her gardens had grown up, and now each garden had their own gardens that they were tending? Was it too late?

No, it was not too late! The Creator Gardener was carefully tilling the soil in this part of her heart garden that caused her the most grief and sorrow—He knew she had tried so diligently to do life differently. He knew she had watered the soil of her heart, drenching the hardness with hot scalding tears day and night. He knew she wanted healing—wholeness of mind, body, and soul. He knew the deep desires of her soul. Her knew her relentless agreement to co-create with God was bringing her into alignment with God the Father—His Father and her Father.

He also knew what His thoughts were for her, and what His plans were for her. Plans to prosper her and not to harm her. Plans to give her hope and a future. Plans to give her an end and expectation for restoration. Plans to bring order out of the chaos. Plans to shine through her. Plans to shine through her brokenness and reflect His Light to the broken and bless the broken in her broken—reflecting His Light into the broken of her own four small heart gardens.

The Creator Gardener smiled. God smiled.

The grief and sorrow were working for her good. Her mourning would be turned to joy, she would be comforted. She would be rewarded for placing her trust and faith in the God who does all things well, giving her hope and an expected end for restoring peace and beauty—quiet soul rest within her borders.

The Creator Gardener sat beside her, weeping, while she sat weeping. Stillness. Quietness. Peace.

Echoing Silence—

Softly she spoke, "My Lord and my God, in this deep valley I worship You. I have found your repetitive forgiveness with every ugly weed I have confessed to you. Your forgiveness has removed the stony hardness from my inner core being. In this valley, instead of stones, I have storehouses full of God's unconditional Love, Mercy, and Grace. I no longer try to be Good Enough. I embrace God's unconditional Love for myself and that is enough. Accepting is restful doing."

"And this that grieves me? —my four small heart gardens? What now?"

Smiling, the Creator Gardener, again, held out His nail-scarred hands.

*Echoing Silence—*she bowed her heart in worship.

She placed four heart gardens into the hands of the Creator Gardener's nail-scarred hands.

She worshiped—*Echoing Silence spoke.*

Quietness—Soul Quietness. Stillness—Knowing He is God. Peace—Resting.

She understands and is learning to embrace and accept God's Unconditional Love for her abiding safe place. His repetitive forgiveness is her space where she gives grace, holding the space of grace for others, leaving her grief and sorrows in His nail-scarred hands.

She is Realigning in God's Creative Design. This is her process to progress.

16

REALIGNING IN GOD'S CREATIVE DESIGN

Embracing Process Not Perfection as the Path to Wholeness

Remember that the renewal of your heart garden is a process—*in every area of life; in order to make progress learned behaviors must be unlearned.* Progress is not perfection. Perfection enslaves and locks the Overcomer of sexual abuse into unrealistic patterns of behavior. God created humans, not robots, and human beings are human, strange creatures of habit who have strengths and weaknesses, and they make mistakes—lots of mistakes. Those mistakes are reminders that every person on the planet has the choice to unlearn the patterns of learned behaviors that brought us to the choices we made that bring regret.

God is a God of Love and His unconditional Love and relentless Forgiveness are His antidotes to shame, blame, guilt, rage, fear, and pain. He is a God who accepts broken messy just the way it is. Broken. Messy. The way I am, just as I am, not perfect. When I embrace and accept this concept, I am transported to realms of grace.

We have traveled many miles, many seasons, many years with Grace as she has taken up her O.A.R. to be a co-creator with God on her healing journey to wholeness. She has had many battles—some ending in glorious victories—others ending in total failure.

What has she done? In good times or bad times, *she has reassessed, readjusted, re-conceptualized, and she has taken all these opportunities to strengthen her inner core being.*

The good times and the victories served to strengthen her resolve and determination to explore more the vastness of wholeness. Her newfound gifts and assets that she was gaining as she brought her thoughts into captivity, expanded her knowledge and understanding of the depths and heights of the Love of God.

There will be bad times throughout the recovery journey. The cycles of crazy eights and learned behaviors that the sexually abused survivor absorbed from early childhood are not going to disappear overnight. Oh, how we wish as in the fairy-tales we read as children, some benevolent, kind, caring, compassionate person would wave a wand, and we'd be instantly transformed with no issues or pain to work through. That, of course, does not happen, and it is a very good thing!

God does not do that either. He could heal us instantly, but because He *is* the kind, caring, benevolent, compassionate, loving Heavenly Father who takes time with each one of us, we are drawn into His love. He fills every single hole in our hearts that abuse left. He alone knows what we need in the exact moment to give the healing we search for.

There is a lot of surgery to be done. No doctor would do the kind of surgery we need all at once. Neither does God. *We would not have time to readjust, re-conceptualize, realign, and change lifelong habits and learned behaviors if He did it all at once.* That would be overwhelming, and we would give up within the beginning first few steps of the journey.

We broke apart piece by piece and that is how we come into wholeness—piece by piece. Yes, we would love to get this over with and move on, and *we do move on.* The journey keeps taking us to new and higher levels. Our comfort zones keep moving out of reach. That is good.

We did not have the opportunity to grow ourselves slowly as children. We allow that little child in us time to grow up. It is exciting and thrilling to see growth in children. We celebrate the growth within as we set our child free to be who God created her to be.

The more we align in God's Creative Design for us, our spiritual growth accelerates. We can grow ourselves as fast as we want to grow in God's grace. There are no limits in Him. We live life to the fullest of our potential when we are realigned in His design and plan. Finding our identity in Christ brings our emotional healing to new and higher levels, and this lays the foundation for lasting transformation. Becoming who God created us to be enables us to daily make the necessary changes to co-create with God.

Change always brings pain. We are moving something that has not moved maybe all through life. This is going to hurt, but we heal in the process.

The pain we feel is our gift to embrace. How does embracing pain release us into healing? We quit denying that the pain belongs to us. This is part of leaving the victim B.E.D. Blame and excuses are so handy to use, we think, until we start making strong advances in recovery, and those means of survival leave us empty and dry. Dealing with anger and realizing how deep our rage has been is scary. It can feel very shaky. That too, is incredibly good. It does not *feel* good because we are desperate for stability. However, this pain shakes off the negative garbage we need to free ourselves from.

We are the only ones who can go into our pain and through it. This is our own personal journey. It is exciting to wake up some morning and actually feel life surging within! It's the same feeling that washes through a new mother as she cuddles her newborn after agonizing pain—pain is forgotten as she gazes into the face of a tiny bit of humanity. She just birthed this baby! She did the hard work! No one else could do what her body just allowed her to do! She surrendered to the pain, and her body knew how to birth this new creation into life.

We rebirth ourselves, giving ourselves new life for the first time! It is a joy we hug close! We are doing this difficult inner work, changing ourselves from the inside out. We think different. We act different. We speak different. We feel different. Because we are different. We are no longer victims. We are no longer just surviving. We are Victors! We are Conquerors! We are Overcomers! We are now thriving in newness of life! We are not just survivors! We are Thrivers! I like the sound of Thrivers! It has a ring to it that takes us far beyond just surviving. We have barely survived through life—*it is time to grow and thrive*!

We began this book in Part 1, looking at the child's need to restore her voice and value. We saw then that this was going to be a process. The basic principles which have been laid out throughout my story are gems and nuggets for you to put into your own toolbox.

You will hone your recovery skills. I look forward to the day I watch you zoom past me running in joyous liberty— set free from the shackles and pain of abuse—free to be the person God created you to be! No longer silenced! Free to live life to your fullest potential knowing you have voice and value—Realigned in God's creative design. You are finding the answers you were searching for! You have taken the steps to recreate your life canvas. You have given yourself value by virtue of the fact that God's truth is your truth. You have learned to value yourself as God values you. You have begun to grieve the losses of childhood and to reconcile to God by embracing pain.

Redefining fears and re-framing learned behaviors was scary work to even consider confronting projected rage, shame, guilt, fear, and pain. You are moving forward, and I am proud of you! It takes so much courage to do this difficult stuff!

Part 2 was our Rebirthing process of rebuilding our foundational principles to become the person God created each of us to be. It was messy, overwhelming, discouraging, terrifying, and extremely hard work to go to the depths of a black abyss and face what we tried to bury and forget. You have made some tough choices!

You are reconnecting to who God created you to be. You are connecting mind, body, and soul. You are looking at your stuff and relinquishing what does not make you whole. You are reconciling to God. Those thought patterns you have grown up with are taking a lot of discipline. I know. We can do this! Choosing is discipline and bringing our thoughts into captivity is how we renew our minds. Renewing our minds in Christ is how we replace and change negative thought patterns. We cannot rush these steps. The refining process is moment by moment as we confront the ruin of our lives, and choosing to act, we step from dark despair into life! Our choices remove the prison walls we have constructed!

Part 3 is our action plan worked out in life. We are realigning to sing God's frequency deep in our souls. Isn't the harmony of your soul and God's just the most beautiful song ever sung? Burning the victim B.E.D. sets the joy bells ringing! Oh, yes! No more *blame, excuses, or denial!* Wow! That B.E.D. had the lumpiest hard mattress ever! If that were not enough to rejoice about, we went to the cross and let Jesus Christ nail all those names and their hurtful masks to the cross with Him. We walked away without names that did not belong to us! He gave us the secret name God gave us before we were born. Mine was Grace. I wonder what your new name is!

Then we found our freedom keys of relentless forgiveness and unconditional love. Those are keys that get a workout daily, but they open the door to hope, mercy, and compassion for those who have wronged us. I thought at the beginning of my journey if I forgave someone, I would not have pain anymore!

I discovered that pain is actually my gift and tool to finding worth, value, and voice. In the process, my soul was re-tuned to sing the frequency of God. Gratitude was the tuning fork God used to enable me to sing in harmony with Him. Don't you just love how your heart is singing in the harmony of light, freedom, and fullness of joy?

Part 4 is our treasure hunt for our true identity. There is gold buried in us all, and we discover that in Christ we find our identity. We reflect His beauty as we co-create with God. We find out that our Heavenly Father is not looking for perfection—He has been waiting to love us just the way we are in all our messy broken. This is how we recreate and co-create God's beauty in us. He shows us how to overcome by using our O.A.R. and become a victor by *taking Ownership, being Accountable, and taking Responsibility* for our own actions. We find wholeness and reflect God's creative image in us when we embrace all our broken messy. God then reflects Himself through our broken by recreating and co-creating in us. Pain is our gift, and when we accept pain as a gift, we have Peace.

In this Peace we co-create with God using our setbacks to be our comebacks. Our relationships will be restored as we relentlessly co-create with God and we accept His repetitive forgiveness and unconditional love for who we are in Christ, not for what we do.

This whole process is our progress to wholeness. We are realigning in God's creative design to be exactly who He created us to be. We are co-creators with Him. We will continue on our journeys until our eyes close in death, and we each, shall hear God say, "Well done, good and faithful Servant, enter into my joys!" And, we shall see God face to face!

ECHOING SILENCE transformed—*ECHOING VOICES* worshiping.

And, God Smiled!

The End to the Start of a New Beginning

AN INVITATION

Actually, there is no END to this book ... This is just the BEGINNING... YOUR beginning...

90-DAY UNHACKABLE VOICE AND VALUE

Unhackable Voice And Value

YOUR JOURNAL TO WHOLENESS

Shari Rickenbach
Certified Unhackable
Coach, Speaker, & Trainer

A Beginning to Restoring Your Voice...And Restoring Your Value....

Shari invites you to join her on her journey through her **90-Day Unhackable Voice and Value Course, A Journal to Wholeness** based on *Echoing Silence from the Child Within* that will be offered at **UnhackableVoiceAndValue.com** or at **ShariRickenbach.com**. As a certified Unhackable Coach, Speaker, and Trainer, Shari coaches one-on-one or in small groups.

Go to her site UnhackableVoiceAndValue.com and **take the free assessment** of your own personal voice and value. You will also discover her introductory **5-Day Unhackable Voice and Value Challenge** to get started on your own journey to wholeness!

BIBLIOGRAPHY

Allender, Dr. Dan B. *The Wounded Heart: Hope for Adult Victims of Childhood Sexual Abuse* (Navpress, 1995).

Betters, Sally. *From Crisis to Compassion: How to Find Empathy, Intimate Connection, and Involvement with Supportive Community* (Author Academy Elite, 2018).

Crabb, Dr. Larry. *Real Change Is Possible—If You're Willing to Start from the Inside Out* (Navpress, 1988).

Deering, Dr. Michelle. *What Mothers Never Tell Their Daughters: 5 Keys to Building Trust, Restoring Connection, and Strengthening Relationships* (Author Academy Elite, 2018).

Duclos, Sandra E. Ph.D. *Waiting for Luigi* (Author Academy Elite, 2019).

Jantz, Gregory L. Ph.D. with Ann McMurray. *Healing the Scars of Emotional Abuse* (Fleming H. Revell, 2004).

Leaf, Dr. Caroline. *The Gift in You: Discover New Life through Gifts Hidden in Your Mind* (Improv, Ltd., 2009).

Leaf, Dr. Caroline. *The Perfect You: A Blueprint for Identity* (Baker Books, 2017).

Leaf, Dr. Caroline. *Switch on Your Brain: The Key to Peak Happiness, Thinking, and Health* (Baker Books, 2013).

Leaf, Dr. Caroline. *Think, Learn, Succeed: Understanding and Using Your Mind to Thrive at School, the Workplace, and Life* (Baker Books, 2018).

Leaf, Dr. Caroline. *Who Switched Off Your Brain? Controlling Toxic Thoughts and Emotions* (Switch on Your Brain International LLC, 2007).

Leaf, Dr. Caroline. *Who Switched Off Your Brain? Solving the Mystery of He Said/She Said* (Improv, Ltd., 2011).

Mellody, Pia with Andrea Wells Miller and J. Keith Miller. *Facing Codependence: What It Is, Where It Comes From, How It Sabotages Our Lives* (Harper One, 2003).

Oberbrunner, Kary. *The Deeper Path: A Simple Method for Finding Clarity, Mastering Life, and Doing Your Purpose Every Day* (Author Academy Elite, 2018).

Oberbrunner, Kary. *Your Secret Name: An Uncommon Quest to Stop Pretending, Shed Labels, and Discover Your True Identity* (Author Academy Elite, 2018).

Samuel, Kirsten. *Choosing a Way Out When the Bottom Isn't the Bottom* (Author Academy Elite, 2017).

Seamands, David A. *Healing for Damaged Emotions* (Victor Books, 1989).

Seamands, David A. *Healing of Memories* (Victor Books, 1985).

Smith, Daphne V. *What's Your Scarlet Letter? Recognize Your Hurts, Release Your Shame, Reclaim Your Voice* (Author Academy Elite, 2018).

Studer, Cathy. *Broken to Beautifully Whole: A Compelling Crusade to Break the Silence, Move through the Trauma, and Heal the Pain* (Author Academy Elite, 2019).

Van Der Kolk, M.D., Bessel. *The Body Keeps the Score: Brain, Mind, and Body in the Healing of Trauma* (Penguin Books, 2014).

Weiss, Laurie and Jonathan B. *Recovery from Co-Dependency: It's Never Too Late to Reclaim Your Childhood* (Health Communications, Inc., 1989).

Whitfield, M.D. Charles L. *Boundaries and Relationships: Knowing, Protecting, and Enjoying the Self* (Health Communications, Inc., 2010).

Whitfield, M.D. Charles L. *Co-Dependence, Healing the Human Condition: The New Paradigm for Helping Professionals and People Recovery* (Health Communications, Inc., 1991).

Whitfield, M.D. Charles L. *Healing the Child Within: Discovery and Recovery for Adult Children of Dysfunctional Families* (Health Communications, Inc., 2006).

ABOUT THE AUTHOR

Shari Rickenbach is an authentic voice for the sexually abused. Her spirit immediately connects with those who have been silenced, marginalized, and shamed by society. Her kind, compassionate, and listening heart has continued to connect with hundreds of listeners wherever she has shared her story. She is a voice for the millions of sex slaves around the world who have no voice!

She is an author, speaker, advocate, and Certified Unhackable Coach and Trainer helping the voiceless become - free from the shackles and pain of abuse – free to be who God created them to be – and free to live life to their fullest potential – Transformed and Restored with Voice and Value. A world-wide door has opened for her to share her story and no longer be invisible about her past. Free to fully live and share is her great joy, privilege, and prayer in bringing this book to your life.

Shari and her husband Lee have been involved in Christian Education ministry for over 40 years. She and her husband are blessed with four children, and six grandchildren.

Connect with Shari at ShariRickenbach.com or UnhackableVoiceAndValue.com.

ON-LINE RESOURCES

Dr. Caroline Leaf's Biographical Material, see:
https://drleaf.com/pages/about-dr-leaf
https://cdn.shopify.com/s/files/1/1810/9163/files/DrLeaf_OneSheet.pdf?v=1588032459

Dr Caroline Leaf's podcasts, blogs, TV shows and You Tube page, see:
https://drleaf.com/pages/podcasts
https://drleaf.com/blogs/news

Dr. Caroline Leaf, product page, see:
https://theswitch.app

Kirsten D. Samuel, see:
https://KirstenDSamuel.com/resources

Made in the USA
Monee, IL
04 July 2021